Understanding Learning ~~Difficulties~~ Differences

Ann Marie Lynch

ORPEN PRESS

Published by
Orpen Press
Upper Floor, Unit B3
Hume Centre
Hume Avenue
Park West Industrial Estate
Dublin 12
email: info@orpenpress.com
www.orpenpress.com

© Ann Marie Lynch, 2024

Paperback ISBN 978-1-78605-152-3
eBook ISBN 978-1-78605-153-0

All rights reserved. No part of this publication may be reproduced, stored in a retrieval system or transmitted in any form or by any means, electronic, mechanical, photocopying, recording or otherwise, for whatever purpose, without the prior written permission of the publisher.

This book is designed to provide information and support to our readers. It is not intended as a substitute for professional advice from psychologists, speech and language therapists, or other professionals. The reader should always consult a relevant professional when required. The content of this book is the sole expression and opinion of the author. No warranties or guarantees are expressed or implied by the publisher's choice to include any of the content in this volume. Neither the publisher nor the author shall be liable for any physical, psychological, emotional, financial or commercial damages, including, but not limited to, special, incidental, consequential or other damages.

To the best of the publisher's knowledge, information in this book was correct at the time of going to press. No responsibility can be taken for any errors.

The publisher has made every effort to contact all copyright holders but if any have been overlooked, they will be pleased to make any necessary arrangements.

Any links or references to external websites or third-party publications should not be construed as an endorsement by the publisher of the content or views of these websites or publications.

Printed in Dublin by SPRINTprint Ltd

Dedicated to the memory of my beautiful and talented big sister and my Dad, one of life's gentle souls.
You'll never be forgotten
Mary Diamond 1965–2023
Jimmie Caulfield 1938–2023

About the Author

Ann Marie Lynch, Mst. BA. H.dip., has been an Additional Educational Needs coordinator in a busy post-primary Dublin school for 20 years. Previous to this she worked as a year head and deputy principal. She has passionately delivered Special Educational Needs lectures in DCU and Trinity College Dublin. She has been involved in many projects that promote the education of others around the area of additional needs, and has participated in national and local advisory groups to advance the educational experiences of students with additional educational needs.

Acknowledgements

I am so grateful to so many people for so many things. I have worked with amazing children and learned much from them and their parents. I have been blessed to work in St Joseph's Secondary School in Rush, a very special place. The staff have shown me how the slightest effort to accommodate an additional need has profound effects. I have learned from my former principal Patricia, who lived by the mantra that all learning takes place in a relationship. Thanks to the management of St Joseph's, Daragh, Judi, Darren and Ciarán, the Student Support Team and Additional Needs Team who work tirelessly to come up with solutions and support to ensure our students' progress and thrive. In doing so, I discovered that we are energised by it. My good friend Paula taught me the importance of slowing down to actually listen to students. Thanks to Yvonne and Emma who demonstrate every day the benefits of positive thinking and good old-fashioned resilience.

To my loving parents, who have been through so much and remain strong no matter what. To Mary and Mike for listening to me ramble on and for setting me straight when needed. I am indebted to my wonderful friends,

'Buddies' and Lynch outlaws – if I named you, I'm afraid I would leave someone out, but you know who you are!

Thank you to my other half, who models how to be true to yourself and to live by your own rules. You make me laugh every day.

Finally, thanks to my little ladies, Faith and Jay Jay, who humour me while I deliver their daily life lessons! They are balls of energy who have given me the greatest source of joy imaginable.

Contents

Acknowledgements v
Abbreviations ix

Introduction................................. 1

1. Evolution and the necessity for diversity 5
2. Nourish your children 8
3. Are labels just for jam jars? 13
4. Accommodations......................... 19
5. Assessment jargon 25
6. What is a spectrum? 37
7. To tell or not to tell 40
8. Home–school relationships 44
9. Homework 54
10. Parenting and teaching................... 57
11. Dyslexia................................ 65
12. Reading 75
13. Spelling and handwriting 84
14. Dysgraphia 94
15. Dyscalculia 98
16. Down's syndrome 108
17. General learning difficulties.............. 111
18. Developmental coordination disorder (DCD)/
    dyspraxia............................. 120

19. ADHD (attention deficit hyperactivity
    disorder) 129
20. Organisation and executive functioning 144
21. Anxiety 154
22. Autism spectrum 167
23. Speech, language and communication. 189
24. Social skills 205
25. Perfectionism 215
26. Study skills 219
27. Dealing with exams 236
28. Keeping your child safe.................... 246
29. A final note 249
Resources 251

Abbreviations

ADHD   attention deficit hyperactivity disorder
AS/ASD   autism spectrum disorder
DCD   developmental coordination disorder/
          dyspraxia
DCU   Dublin City University
DSM   *Diagnostic and Statistical Manual of Mental
          Disorders*
GAI   General Ability Index
GLD   general learning difficult
IEP   Individual Education Plan
MGLD   mild general learning difficulty
OT   occupational therapist
PE   physical education
SPD   sensory processing disorder

Introduction

It was the day of my entrance test into secondary school and I was so excited. The prospect of new friends and adventures was thrilling. It was my debut into the adolescent world. We were asked to write an essay, a diary entry entitled 'The day in the life of a house mouse'. Bursting with ideas, I let my pen loose on the page. At the end of the test we were advised to 'look over' our work. My heart sank. I contemplated not handing it up, as it was full of blobs and misspellings. The handwriting was, as I had been told many times, 'a disgrace'. For years I struggled with the fact that despite my best efforts, my handwriting was messy and embarrassing. I would attempt to outsmart my teachers by making my writing so small that they couldn't make out the difference between an *e* or an *a* or an *i*, simply because I hadn't a clue if I should be using an *a*, *e*, or *i* in many of the spellings. Orally, I knew I was as bright as my peers, yet this damn writing business kept letting me down!

Now you might be expecting me to share horror stories of being hit or scolded or underestimated. Quite the contrary. While I remained embarrassed by my poor spelling and handwriting, I was surrounded by teachers who had high expectations for me. Had I been born into a different Ireland, say 20 years previously, my experiences and life chances would have been devastatingly different. Yes, there were plenty of references to poor spelling and tidy work, but my results always reflected an acknowledgement of the content and quality of the work, as opposed to some archaic glorification and obsession with spelling. I was self-assured in the knowledge that intelligence had no relation to spelling or pretty writing and had little tolerance for those who still held on to such ridiculous and outdated concepts. There are unfortunately many adults who did not have such positive student experiences. They have had their confidence shattered by simple learning differences, compounded with flippant teacher, parent or peer remarks. My first piece of advice: the only person who should joke about poor spelling/handwriting is the person with the poor spelling/handwriting!

In school, particularly in Geography, I loved to teach other students. If anybody didn't get their revision homework done, I'd be happy to give them a five-minute summary. Enough to bluff the teacher into thinking they had done it at home. So, naturally, becoming a teacher was my main ambition. Off I went to university, discovered spell check and never looked back! Yes, I had to spend longer proofreading my work or badger my sister or friends to proofread it for me, but this never really seemed to bother me. I liked learning.

As I worked in a designated 'disadvantaged school' for my first eight years of teaching, I soon learned that the classrooms were full of struggling readers and writers. I spent my time as a deputy principal, but soon fate would have it that I went back to college and trained as a special education teacher.

A few years later, fate also had it that my eldest daughter got a diagnosis of dyspraxia and my youngest a diagnosis of dyslexia. Diagnosis – funny word, isn't it? Full of implications, like there is something medically wrong with you. While I had studied extensively, read widely and congratulated myself on being very 'experienced' in the area of learning differences, nothing provided a steeper learning curve than the journey I continue to take with my two vibrant, wonderful and powerful young daughters.

I have approached the writing of this book from many angles – the embarrassed and ashamed teen, the concerned and overanxious parent, and the teacher who holds high expectations for her students. It is not an academic book. If you are looking for references to the latest ground-breaking research, you need to know that there won't be any! While writing this book I have drawn not only on the many courses I have taken with Trinity College Dublin and the National Council of Special Education, but more importantly on the experiences and journeys I have had the privilege of sharing with my students and children. I will share versions of what has worked for them and what has worked for me.

While there may be some chapters you feel are not relevant for you or your child, nevertheless I would urge you to read all the chapters. Most learning difficulties do not fit neatly into one pigeonhole or another. 'Co-morbidity' is the term used when students have two or more perceived learning differences. Rather than saying they have a few different diagnoses, I feel it is a more accurate description to say that when you know your child has a learning difficulty, there will be different degrees of difficulties. It is inaccurate to slot them under one umbrella. They may share traits from lots of different umbrella diagnoses, with different degrees of severity. You will notice throughout the book that I refer to 'learning difficulties' and 'learning differences'. A child may present as having difficulties, but it may be helpful to view how the child learns as different. Children are so individual in their talents and needs. It is wise to always keep the individual at the centre of everything.

I'm not a scientist, but I will be sharing with you my understanding of the underlying reasons for some learning differences. I apologise if I offend some for oversimplifying into Ladybird versions, but I can only share with you my own interpretations. We've all heard the stories of how Einstein was regarded as having a severe learning disability. We now know there is a thing called neurodiversity. While some might say it's political correctness, it is simply an accurate description. The different ways students learn is simply down to neurodiversity – the wiring of the brain is not standard. Anything away from the norm or the majority is not a defect. It is just a minority group.

1

Evolution and the necessity for diversity

In brain scans, it is clear that there are differences between someone regarded as 'neurotypical' and someone with dyslexia, autism spectrum (AS) or attention deficit hyperactivity disorder (ADHD). Differences, but not a defect, illness nor anything that requires a cure. Quite the contrary. We know that evolution is mind-numbingly brilliant. Things that are required are kept ... and things that are not required are dispensed with.

Diversity should be valued not because it is ethically or morally right, but because we need it. It's essential to our survival. The genes for autism, ADHD, etc. are not mistakes but actually a superior evolutionary strategy. One of the genes found in people with ADHD is known as the novelty-seeking gene. Some will see it as impulsivity, making school difficult, or you could view it as a burning curiosity upon which all ground-breaking knowledge is built on. The genes associated with autism may also be regarded as contributing to society, as those who have them have natural dispositions and an awareness of sensory information such as smell, taste and hearing, and they frequently have exceptional memory or logical abilities. The ability to block out the bigger picture and focus on small details is the perfect scenario for great discoveries. On the flip side, those with dyslexia may find that they do the opposite of focusing on detail – they see the whole picture. They may be problem-solvers and outside-the-box solution-finders simply because they *don't* have tunnel vision. These genes remain in the gene pool because they are useful.

We know the brain controls every single thing we do. Our memories, our worries, our joy, our learning, our perceptions. It controls essentials like eating, sleeping and breathing. The brain has two sides. The left is where all the language, science, maths and logic takes place. The right is where creativity, art, music, holistic intuition and problem-solving takes place. The right side of the brain controls the left side of the body and the left side of the brain controls the right side of the body. While the brain is the command centre, it needs its minions – the neurons – to do the work. Neurons send messages to the body to do the things listed above. When we learn something, we are connecting one neuron to another. The more we practise a new skill or piece of knowledge, the more strength we are giving to the pathway between these two neurons. Practise this skill enough and it becomes automated. We are not born being able to ride a bike or knit or type, but with repetition, it becomes automated. *This is why when a student struggles with a skill or a new spelling, overlearning and repeated practice, while frustrating, is highly effective.*

One basic piece of advice: if you suspect your child or student may have a learning difficulty, get all their senses checked. This is important to rule out possible poor sight or hearing as the root cause of any difficulties or learning gaps.

So many learning differences are neurological and genetic. It is something the child is born with. It should never be viewed as coming from 'his side of the family' or 'her side of the family'. It is extremely important to not see a learning difference as something that needs to be cured.

2

Nourish your children

In recent years we have been bombarded with researched based advice on what we should eat and drink. TV shows, magazines, social media, it's everywhere. So I'm not going to attempt going into detail on this huge topic. I am however going to just outline a few key points.

Hydration

Make sure your child stays hydrated. If you have a basil plant and deprive it of water, it will wilt. Give it some water and it will be revived a few hours later. You will literally see it revitalise. Our brains are exactly like that – not enough water and your brain wilts. It simply cannot learn. Fizzy drinks are not hydration – in fact they are the opposite. It is best not to let your children have them on a daily basis.

Sleep

Babies get all frustrated and agitated if they are tired. The same is true for children, teens and adults. Your children must get enough sleep. The recommended hours are as follows:

- *Children*: 10–12 hours sleep
- *Teens*: 9–10 hours sleep
- *Adults*: 8 hours sleep

If your child is not getting enough sleep, you need to get to the bottom of this. There is always a reason for not getting enough sleep. Is there a poor night-time routine with screens just before bedtime? Is there a set time for bed or a haphazard approach? Are they going to bed on time but worried about something? I had one teen who said she kept waking up at 4 a.m. We delved into it a little more.

'What do you do when you wake up at 4 a.m.?'
'I check my phone to see what time it is.'
'Is that all you do with your phone?'
'I check for any messages.'

Get the phones out of the children's bedroom. If you encounter difficulties doing this, then one solution is to turn off the wi-fi. However many children are now on data plans. You will need to get them to hand over the phone an hour before bedtime. They may give out, but you must hold strong on this. My daughter struggled with sleeping. It doesn't get fixed overnight. I'd go up to her room and she'd have a notebook or sketchpad filled with drawings and buildings and all sorts of creative masterpieces. Her brain and neurons were lit up like a

Christmas tree. Hardly conducive to sleep. Figuring out the root of the sleep difficulties may take a little time to explore, but it is essential to try and give them some strategies for getting asleep and staying asleep. Would reading a book at night help? Are they drinking water too late? Do they need a specified time in the evening, say 10 minutes at 6:00 p.m., to off-load their worries. This may prevent the tired brain from going on to catastrophize a small issue and consequently keep them awake later that night.

Meditation recordings or audio books can be useful. One teen shared that 'Those apps are so boring – they send me to sleep every time.' Of course you then have to have a device in the room to use these!

Diet

I'm only going to summarise what you already know: rubbish food, rubbish mood! Rubbish mood – poor learning.

Try to avoid fad diets. There are lots of government guidelines out there to follow that will ensure your child is nourished. Bring them shopping with you and get them to pick out what they like. Lots of students with learning differences find trying new foods daunting. Getting cross with them is the natural reaction but rarely successful. Their diet may be very limited. My advice is to keep chipping away. Every now and then something new will become accepted by your child and you can add it to the list. It's a slow process but keep calm and keep persistent in the quest to introduce new and nourishing foods.

Sugar bad! Enough said! Before I come across as the party pooper, you need to know that all parents struggle with modern living. Everywhere you turn there are treats for children. Everything is supersized, and even when you ask for a small cone, you are presented with enough heaped ice cream to feed three. You could always scoop some off, but then what was supposed to be an act of giving turns into you being the evil parent who put half their ice cream in the bin ... argh! All you can do is your best, but we have a responsibility to nourish our children and as teachers we have a duty to reinforce this message. The brain needs to be nourished by protein, vitamins, minerals, carbohydrates and oils. Limiting the rubbish is a tough job but it's our responsibility.

Exercise

Again, you already know the advice on exercise. Some parents are blessed with the child who loves sport and they are dragging their children in every night sweaty and dirty, puffing and panting. Lucky you. Others have children who are happy to lounge on the couch all day or who are simply addicted to screens. If this is your child, well you have to work with them to understand that exercise is essential and expected. They can choose what they like but they must choose something. So many of my students simply hate team sports. The idea of physical contact can be terrifying for them, especially if they have sensory issues. The idea of not being picked for the team can be soul-destroying. Why would they subject themselves to that humiliation?

Well, *exercise* is something quite distinct from *sport*. Try any of the following:

- Bringing the dog for a walk
- Going for a run
- Doing a couch-to-5k programme
- Joining a gym
- Following one of the millions of YouTube exercise videos

Whatever interests them! Getting a buddy to exercise with is definitely helpful, so it is great if you could link with other parents in similar situations. It would make it more sociable. No one said parenting was easy, but as exercise is essential for the brain to function properly, do your best to encourage your children to exercise regularly.

3

Are labels just for jam jars?

Assessments are very useful and even necessary for many students. To assess or not to assess? – that is the question parents always ask. It's a very individual question that cannot be broadly answered. For example, we need to know if a student has dyslexia if we are to provide a tailored educational programme for them. However, so often teachers presume students are no good at reading because they were labelled as dyslexic.

Do you think children should be labelled? Ridiculous question, isn't it? Of course they shouldn't. I've spoken to endless parents who have chosen not to get an assessment because they do not want their children labelled with some term or condition. There are stereotypical images that come with each diagnosis. Surely children should not be labelled. While I understand this argument, I have to tell you that I am the first to suggest that students should be assessed if there are indicators of a learning need. Both my daughters were assessed and given a diagnosis, or label, and I have no regrets, but ultimately it is a parent's or guardian's decision.

When some people think of dyslexia, they might think of a person who has difficulties reading, but that is not always the case. My daughter is a great reader – it's spellings that are the issue. I hear parents saying, 'He couldn't have dyspraxia, sure isn't he great at sport' or 'She crawled really early', or 'Autism? But he can speak perfectly well and he's very affectionate.'

Assessment and consequent diagnosis are only appropriate when we park the stereotypes. To ignore a learning need is to just stick your head in the sand. Students with dyslexia are as bright as their peers. They need to be given that crucial reason as to why their handwriting sucks or why they can't keep up. I've seen teens who had a late diagnosis suddenly regain their self-confidence and self-belief because the assessment provided them with a reason why, an answer to the puzzle. Instead of panicking about the teacher asking them to read, they now have the authority to walk up to their teacher and confidently request some sort of differentiation. They may ask to get the reading the night before if they are expected to read aloud in class, or request handing in an assignment by email. Maybe someday all schools will allow all students to use assistive technology regardless of any 'labels'.

For the moment, getting a diagnosis of developmental coordination disorder/dyspraxia (DCD), autism, dysgraphia, etc. allows the student to access appropriate help and accommodations. Assistive technology can be used to record answers, send homework by email, take photos of the board, etc. and therefore avert hours of stress trying to handwrite work, losing bits of pages or missing bits of instructions for homework.

I have seen students experience enormous relief when they were diagnosed with autism, as they knew they were 'different' and now at least they had the answer and could access the world of support groups and relevant information.

Speaking from a personal point of view, unless we have an actual diagnosis, sometimes we as parents can be particularly hard on our children. Many parents have confided that after a diagnosis, they felt enormous guilt. Guilt for having been hard on their children about spellings, constantly forgetting things or for having messy handwriting, reprimanding their children for not trying hard enough. The diagnosis can be the 'ah-ha' moment. Now don't get me wrong, you will still have to keep working on the spellings or switch from handwriting to typing, or whatever is recommended to support your child. But now, from a parental point of view, your patience threshold instantly increases and therefore your relationship with your child improves.

I'm not a psychologist, but I think children need time to develop. Children have different spurts and pauses of development. Some difficulties can be confidently diagnosed early on. Some difficulties may just need support and time for development.

We all have traits of this and that – should we all get assessed? Of course not. You only need to seek a 'diagnosis' if the observed difficulty is holding the child back or causing them some distress. It isn't a problem unless it is in fact causing problems. We shouldn't be going around looking to slap labels on children but sometimes children need to have a difficulty named so it they can be given a targeted and tailored intervention.

Learning differences can be very discrete, and children use strategies to overcome and manoeuvre around their difficulties. Students with dyslexia who also have a high IQ often underperform in reading and writing tests, yet still fall within the average range, so everyone thinks they're grand. They're not grand! These students, who should be high achievers, have to work really hard just to get average grades. They may never get a diagnosis of dyslexia, leaving their self-esteem damaged as they wonder why they struggle with spelling or reading or whatever the difficulty may be. This is underperformance and a loss of human potential. Standardised tests in reading, writing and general school exams should reflect a student's full-scale IQ. Educational psychology assessments measure this full-scale IQ and measure students' literacy and numeracy scores against it. The discrepancy in scores will flag a specific learning difficulty.

If you feel there is something different in your child or student, you need to take note of exactly what that is. Is it social, physical or relating to literacy and numeracy? Measure their written answers against their verbal ability. Once you are satisfied that you have evidence that there is a difficulty, but you can't put your finger on, discuss it with someone else. If you are a parent, chat with the teacher. If you are a teacher, chat with the parent. I felt that my daughter's handwriting was a little off. I asked her teacher about her progress.

'She's wonderful, great, bright, getting good scores.'

I asked, 'Would you say her handwriting matches her verbal ability?'

It was a very specific question and the answer confirmed my suspicions. Once we had completed an assessment and established DCD, the school provided targeted intervention and the results were amazing. The more opinions you get the better. Maybe an intervention can be made before you decide on getting an assessment. *See if there are any improvements with interventions prior to going off to get an assessment. Allow time for development.*

Not all students who display learning differences require an assessment, but after consultations have taken place with parents, teachers and most importantly the student, it may be obvious that an assessment would be helpful. Always ask why do we want an assessment? What do we hope to get out of it? Assessments are expensive if you get them done privately. You may have to wait a long time if you go through the public system. Here's my take on that: if you spot the signs of a learning difference, have a good chat with the child and get them to explain it to you. With their consent, target the area of difficulty with some sort of programme or support strategies. Give a little time for development and see if they difficulties still remain. Then, if in doubt, check it out. It is very cruel to have a student coping without appropriate support throughout their whole school lives, not knowing why they are having difficulties and internalising self-doubt. If you choose to get your child assessed there is a chance the assessment will show that your child doesn't have a learning difficulty. If that is the case, as a parent you may feel you've wasted money. Not at all. An assessment shows learning preferences. It shows you which subjects and consequently which careers your child is likely to thrive in. It shows you areas that require focus of course, but, more importantly, it shows you areas of strength.

In my experience the public system clinicians are highly effective and accurate. The only difficulty is the waiting time. So my advice here is chop-chop! The sooner you get on the list the better. There's no point saying 'Oh well, the waiting list is really long.' Your turn will eventually come. I know some parents who felt their child had a learning difficulty and this was confirmed by the school – they sought an assessment and were told there would be a ridiculous amount of time to wait. They threw their hands up in disgust. Before they knew it we were sitting having the same conversation two years later. If they had just got on the list promptly at the start of the journey, they would have been seen already. The public system can be frustrating – who assesses, who do you go to first? Your GP or local health clinic is always a good starting point and they should be able to guide you on how to go about getting an assessment. The schools have access to psychologists. Ask the school if you feel they would qualify for an assessment. The Health Service Executive have excellent psychologists, occupational therapists, physiotherapists, and speech and language therapists. Request an assessment here. If the waiting lists are too long, ask your GP or school if they have names of clinicians who work privately. The important thing is to keep pursuing it until you get what your child requires.

4

Accommodations

Accommodations is a term we use to describe what we put in place to level the playing field for our students with learning differences. We can discuss with the student which accommodations they find useful. Table 1 provides a list of some accommodations that a teacher can implement in their classroom. There may also be accommodations that a student may be entitled to at state exam level. Each country will have their own system of accommodations. The SEC (State Examination Commission) in Ireland decides on what criteria is required for a student to be entitled to accommodation in the state exams. The additional needs coordinator in the school will be able to advise students, parents and teachers.

TABLE 1: AVAILABLE ACCOMMODATIONS

Difficulty	Accommodation
Writing difficulties	• Word processor • Speech-to-text software • Use a scribe (a person to write what they say)
Spelling and grammar difficulties	• Spelling and grammar waiver
Reading difficulties	• Text-to-speech software • Reader for state exams • Reader pen
Physical difficulties	• Use a helper for practical elements • Exemption from parts of an exam • Specialist equipment or assistive technology • Magnified/Braille versions of papers or worksheets • Recording devices • Sign language interpreter • Rest breaks
Writing speed	• Extra time to finish class work or use of assistive technology and recording devices
In-class copying from the board	• Take a photo with an iPad or smartphone
Language difficulties	• Exemption from languages • Spelling and grammar waivers
Emotional/behavioural difficulties	• Movement breaks • Separate centres for exams

There are a whole host of accommodations your child may be entitled to. In fact, you may find that you are entitled to financial support or tax exemptions. While it is important to put in place all that your child or student is entitled to, it is equally important to make sure you implement only what is genuinely helpful.

Quite often we can insist on putting some form of accommodation in place – demanding our entitlements – only to find that it doesn't in fact assist the student, but further encumbers them. Lots of students thrive with a laptop for example. On the flip side, I have lots of students who only use a laptop at home, as they find it frustrating to use it in class. One student described how he gets delayed when his laptop takes a while to start up and the class carries on without him. At the end of class he loses out on leaving the classroom with his friends as he has to unplug it and pack it up into the laptop bag. Teachers can make small accommodations here by allowing them a few minutes before the end of class to pack up, but of course they may be missing helpful summaries at the end of class. Students who have dyspraxia can benefit greatly from using a laptop but for some their finger dexterity is insufficient.

After consultation with the student and deciding on what helps and works for them, the parent and teacher can go about implementing any of the above accommodations. There is no law against implementing any accommodations but we should be careful not to implement an accommodation that they are unlikely to get in the state examinations. We can make them dependent on this type of accommodation and then it's whipped away when it matters most. We should always strive to ensure we accommodate learning differences so that the student can reach their full potential. At primary level, appropriate accommodations can ensure that they can keep up with the pace of work in the class. It can ensure that they are not disadvantaged by spending hours of their time on homework. At second level we cannot allow them to become dependent on any accommodation that they will not be entitled to when they get to the stage of state exams. In the Irish context, the State Examination Commission issues a booklet each year stating clearly the criteria for such accommodations. I have read assessments by clinicians giving recommendations for accommodations that simply don't exist within the structure of state examinations. These can change from year to year so you need to keep up to date with these. In the Irish context, you can keep up to date with these accommodations by going to the following website. There will be a drop-down menu called reasonable accommodation.

https://www.examinations.ie/schools

The entitlements are based on reading/writing standard scores (the school will have these), or writing/reading speeds, etc. Link closely with the additional needs coordinator in the school to get advice on what accommodations the student is likely to be entitled to at state examination level. Even if the student isn't entitled to the accommodation in state exam situations, a student may still choose to use this accommodation in the classroom just to make school life a little easier. I know for example when the writing gets too much for students and they simply run out of time for homework, the only way to manage the work load is to use speech to text. It saves a night of stress. Sometimes it is obvious that a student will be entitled to a specific accommodation. If your student clearly has a sight difficulty, they will need the material magnified in some way. If a student has an enormous amount of spelling mistakes, say more than 8 in every 100 words, then they are likely to be entitled to a spelling and grammar waiver and the teacher could implement this waiver when correcting their assignments. If the student is in anyway borderline in an entitlement, then they should never become completely dependent on any one accommodation. They should use speech to text or typing for example if their handwriting is difficult to read or very slow, but they should also use the pen for a good percentage of the time, just in case they do not qualify for the accommodation. Discussions need to be had with teachers, parents and students around this situation. Teachers could give a mark with a spelling and grammar waiver and a mark without. Getting appropriate accommodation for a learning difficulty is tricky business. To summarise, my recommendation is:

- Link with the student and figure out what accommodations they would find genuinely helpful. Give them options and reassure them that they are in control.
- Class teachers and parents should link with the additional needs coordinator and discuss what accommodations they feel would benefit the child given their level of need, difficulty or difference.
- Try out appropriate accommodations and give each accommodation time and practice. Review how they get on with the different accommodations. Implement any strategy that will help your student or child keep up with their peers and reach their full potential.
- At second level, ensure you are up to date with the state examinations criteria for accommodation. Check that you are not making a student dependent on an accommodation they will not be entitled to at state examination level. What underpins the spirit of reasonable accommodation is the idea of making things fair. Your child will not be given marks simply

because they have an additional need, however an accommodation should be implemented to offset any potential or likely underachievement arising from their learning difference.

5

Assessment jargon

In Chapter 3 we discussed the topic of getting an assessment and ultimately it is a parental/guardian decision that should be guided by communications with the student and the school. There is no right or wrong decision. If you do choose to get an assessment, then the jargon in the clinical or educational assessment can be a little off-putting. Bear with me as once we explain a few terms, the assessment becomes much more informative.

- GAI: General Ability Index: Measuring cognitive abilities. It gives a general indication if the child is cognitively functioning at an above average range or average range. The child may be dealing cognitive challenges which are categorised into mild, moderate, severe or profound cognitive learning ability. This type of assessment checks things such as *working memory*, *processing speed* and *reasoning*.

- Processing speed: Cognitive speed. How long it takes us to process a piece of information or work something out.
- Executive function: Working memory, flexible thinking and impulse control
- Verbal, non-verbal: The ability to think in words or symbols.
- Attainment tests: There are attainment tests in literacy and numeracy. Assessments can measure *handwriting speed*, *motor skills* and *attention*. They should broadly match the GAI in terms of scores.

I want to remind you that I'm not a clinician or psychologist. So I'll be explaining the jargon in terms that make sense to me. I'm afraid I like the Ladybird version of everything as opposed to medically or scientifically acceptable definitions. Apologies if you find I over-simplify some terms.

There are many different types of assessments, but the following are the most common:

- Educational psychologist assessment
- Occupational therapist assessment
- Speech, language and communication assessment

Input is given from parents, teachers and, more importantly, the student. Testing gives us an idea of how our child or student should perform in relation to their peers. Administration instructions are given to ensure that all students sit the tests in the same conditions. By far the most important point here is that these assessments also highlight the personal strengths of the students. Perhaps their visual and spatial abilities are superior even if their reading scores are well below average. So they may not be great readers, but they could be brilliant designers. Parents can get caught up on the low scores and overlook the strengths that are also highlighted in these assessments. Most assessments do not capture how happy a child is, nor do they capture the personality traits that determine if they will be happy into the future, for example kindness, resilience, sense of humour, ability to bring joy to those around them. Assessments do however provide the answers to lots of questions. They will guide the parents and professionals on the best path to supporting the child.

Each assessment will have different sections or areas of assessment. When a student has completed the assessment, the professional will then crunch the numbers and give you the results of each section in a written report. These results will indicate if the student is falling below, within or above the average range for their age. Basically, is the area being tested (such as processing speed or working memory or reading etc.) an area of strength or an area of challenge?

There are no A, B or C grades in an assessment. No matter what is being measured – General Ability Index, reading age or spelling – the measurements are often presented in terms of *standardised scores*, *reading ages*, *percentiles* or *stanines*.

READING THE ASSESSMENT SCORES

Standardised scoring

If you look this one up, you will see lots of information about standard deviations, blah blah blah. I'm afraid I'm just going to offer you my simple interpretation again.

When a student takes a standardised test, they get a 'raw' score. Their age is then taken into account and the figure is converted into a standard score. If they get bang on 100, they are average. If they score between 85 and 120, they are regarded as being within the average range. If they score below 85, an intervention of support in that area is required (see Table 2).

TABLE 2: STANDARDISED TEST SCORES

Score	Description
<69	Very low
70–84	Low
85–89	Low average
90–110	Average
111–120	High average
121–131	Superior

Reading ages

Should be banned! They are soul-destroying and counterproductive. Obviously, this is just my own personal opinion. Some practitioners may find them useful. I'm just always afraid my students may see these scores. After all, we could argue that they are entitled to their own personal information. A sixteen-year-old will find it hard to be motivated if they see they have a reading age of 10.

Percentiles

This is a type of ranking that places the student on a scale from 1 to 100. Bang in the middle is 50. So if the report gives a percentile of 50, then the student is at the average level. In other words, it is a ranking according to what is average for the student's peers. If you have an assessment that says the student is in the 1st percentile, this means that 99% of the student's peers would do better than them. Or indeed if they are in the 99th percentile, then only 1% of the population at their age would do better than them. (See Table 3.)

TABLE 3: PERCENTILE SCORES

Score	Description
0–2	Very low
3–10	Low
11–24	Low average
25–75	Average
76–90	High average
91–100	Superior

STENS

This scale goes from 1 to 10, with 5 being the middle. A score of:

- 1–3 will require a support intervention
- 4–7 is average
- 8–10 is above average

OTHER ASSESSMENT TERMINOLOGY

There are many different subsets and elements to the different types of assessments. Things that frequently come up as difficulties or strengths are:

Executive functions

This is a group of mental skills we use to get things done:

- Working memory
- Flexible thinking
- Impulse control

Obviously, a student who is constantly forgetting things is displaying signs of poor working memory. A student with ADHD may have impulse difficulties. A student with autism may struggle with flexible thinking. It is important to know that poor impulse control, poor working memory or inflexibility are not linked to intelligence. It has been my experience that poor impulse control is often simply linked to immaturity.

1. Working memory

Let's say someone gives you the entry code to a door. You have to hold that number in your head long enough to punch it in and open the door. Then you can get rid of it. You are holding this information in your short-term memory. This is your working memory. Imagine a teacher gives a student five instructions to complete a task. If the student has a poor working memory, they may remember only two, so they cannot complete the task. Poor working memory really affects learning, as holding information in our heads long enough to use it is required in lots of subjects, like maths and reading. There is also auditory memory (remembering what you hear) and visual memory (remembering what you see).

Working memory is linked to attention. Lots of lessons are building blocks – teachers explain step by step, keeping the students hooked bit by bit. If a student's working memory is poor, they may lose some of the steps. The student feels lost and so they lose interest.

Some students have super auditory memories, but for others who don't, too much teacher talk is just white noise ... blah, blah, blah ... so to speak. If learning is like building blocks, then students need to remember all the previous blocks as a foundation for the next new block. If their visual working memory is poor, they may struggle to recognise and hold patterns. Recognising patterns is a skill needed in maths, but also in learning to read. When students are decoding a word, they have to hold the sounds of each letter long enough in their head to crack the whole word. Students should eventually be sight reading. Sight reading means recognising words because they have seen them lots of times before and are not having to constantly decode words. This is what makes a fluent reader. Working memory affects comprehension – a student will have to remember the story as a whole to answer the questions. They will also need to remember key snippets in order to draw conclusions and understand.

The good news is that working memory is like a muscle that can be exercised. There are lots of strategies that can be used to strengthen the working memory

THINGS TO ASSIST THE WORKING MEMORY

Chunk information

Both parents and teachers will need to chunk information. Don't present the whole mountain to the student.

Present the first few steps and then the next few steps and before you know it, you've climbed the mountain. It may require teachers to break up blocks of text into bullet-point paragraphs. Praise every step of the way. Don't give six instructions: give two instructions, then two more and then two more.

What goes in must come out

Children have a wonderful habit of nodding in all the right places. 'Do you understand?' is always followed by 'Yes'. What they really might be thinking is 'this is torture': if they say 'No', then you'll go over it all again. If they say 'Yes', then the hope is you'll move on. You can't expect children/teens to be mature enough to say, 'No, I don't understand, and I'd like you to go over that again.' Checking for understanding is important. If the information goes in, then at that moment get the student to regurgitate it in some way. Explain it back to you. Draw a bullet point list of the main points. Do a mind map. The process of information in, information out somehow acts as a hook. It also ensures that you don't move on before that foundation block is mastered.

Games

There are lots of fun games that help working memory. You can find puzzles online that have little cards with pictures and bits of information. You can even make your own with simple pictures. The student gets a minute to look at it, then you quiz them on what they can remember from the card. What colour was the boy's hat? How many flowers had the girl in her hand?

Did you ever play 'I went to the shop and I bought X'? You take turns with each person adding another item to the list. You could even play card games like Go Fish. Working memory is like a muscle that can be built up. These are working memory workouts.

Notes

Get students to come up with strategies that work for them. This is particularly important for older students. During class they should be jotting down important bits of information along the way. Working memory is often referred to as a mental sticky note. If their mental sticky note is letting them down, they should use a physical one. Jotting down bits of information as they go will help. The notes don't have to be neat, or even make sense to others – they won't be keeping it. They simply help to keep them focused along the way.

Highlighters

When reading for comprehension, a highlighter should be an older student's best friend. Highlighting key points means they don't need to store them mentally. Younger students will need a lot of practice and support with this as they have a tendency to just colour the page leaving out the little words like and or it. They need to be taught to think about the content and if it's important before they highlight it, otherwise it just becomes a colouring exercise with no cognitive engagement.

   Strategies for improving memory are discussed in more detail in the chapter to follow on study skills.

2. Flexible thinking

This is the ability to look at difficulties from lots of different perspectives and solve them. Being too rigid and dedicated to one way of looking at things can be quite debilitating. A student with poor flexible thinking can get stuck in tunnel vision. Socially they may have difficulty with friends as they refuse to change games or just go with the flow. This comes across as stubborn or uncooperative. It may also have an impact on academic subjects. Take Maths as an example. They may find it difficult to change from one way of approaching a problem even if an alternative method is more efficient or accurate.

3. Impulse control

This is the ability to have instant reflection before acting on impulse. It requires the student to have attention and focus. This allows them to instantly imagine the consequences of their actions before they act. It also allows them to manage their emotions, and control their ability to concentrate. If they are unable to control their behaviour by using impulse control, habits that are acceptable when they are a child continue into their teens, where these behaviours are now unacceptable.

Processing speed

No matter how information gets into a student's brain, they then have to process it. They may *hear* teachers or parents giving them instructions, but they then need to *process* it in order to act on that information.

Students with slow processing speeds may seem indecisive, but what is really happening is that they are contemplating the different options before they make a decision. The difficulty lies in the fact that life is very fast-paced and parents and teachers may just hurry things along by making decisions for them. This leads to students being deprived of developing independence skills.

In class, students are given lots of instructions and information. Take the scenario where a student is processing a piece of information or an instruction. They totally understand the information. It is not an intelligence issue, but it just takes longer to process. The pace of the class, however, is very fast and before they have completely processed the information the teacher has moved on to the next piece of information. The student decides not to finish processing the first piece of information so they can try to grasp the next bit of information being thrown at them, in the hope that they will be given the time to process it this time. Teachers and parents need to decide if extra time is needed for the coursework or the amount of coursework should be reduced in order to facilitate students with a slow processing speed.

A FINAL NOTE ON ASSESSMENTS

A very important thing to remember is that an assessment is a picture in time. It is a snapshot. If a student isn't feeling well, is feeling anxious or, indeed, decides to be uncooperative on the day of the assessment, then the scores will be inaccurate. I've read plenty of assessments of students made when they were just seven or eight years old – a snapshot in time at a particular age. The picture the assessment paints is often very far removed from the teen I'm eventually working with. Students can improve significantly. The assessments, in general, give very good indicators of difficulties and strengths. They highlight areas where students need support and areas where they are likely to thrive. The recommendations at the end of assessments are truly invaluable and should be considered regularly.

6

What is a spectrum?

Whether stated on an assessment or not, if we have established that our child or student has learning differences we must tailor support to the individual. When we hear the word 'spectrum' we automatically think of autism. But *spectrum* is a word in its own right. Here's how the *Cambridge English Dictionary* defines it:

'A range of different positions between two extreme points.'

Teachers often say to me that they have a student who is 'struggling'. The area of concern could be academic, social or physical. We then need to get a bit more scientific. If you devise a sheet with areas of concern and get them to plot a position between two points, then we get a less subjective statement than 'struggling'.

In relation to learning differences, the term 'spectrum' is applicable in all perceived areas of learning differences and not exclusively to people with autism.

Take the traits of any given label – excuse me, diagnosis! – and plot your child on that line. Just to note: the scales in the figures below are not three-point scales. They are continuous lines that extend gradually between two extremes. Plot your child anywhere along the lines.

For example, let's take the common traits of dyslexia:

Reading at an age-appropriate level

Cannot read independently	Needs a little help	Can read independently

←——————————————————————————→

Spelling

Making large amounts of errors	Making a few errors	Making no errors

←——————————————————————————→

Organisation

Extremely disorganised	Needs a little support	Highly organised

←——————————————————————————→

Handwriting

Completely illegible	Fairly legible	Perfectly legible

←——————————————————————————→

By doing this exercise you are acknowledging that no two children are the same. You will then be able to identify specifically the areas that need work. It is really nice for students to see that 'usually' students with dyslexia (as in this example) have difficulty with this or that ... but look, you don't have a difficulty in this area. It is also good to establish which areas they do have difficulties with and focus on one or two of these. Maybe a support teacher is spending time on developing reading skills or maths skills but you know your student or child doesn't have a difficulty in this area. Pick a specific area and plot it on the line below. If there is 'no difficulty' then there is no point wasting energy or time on things they do not have difficulties with. If you find yourself plotting closer to the 'severe' end then this should be a priority area for support.

No difficulty   Severe difficulty
←—————————————————————————————————→

There are many different traits for any given diagnosis. Just because your student or child has a diagnosis of dyspraxia doesn't mean they automatically have all the traits. The spectrum is a really useful way of understanding the degree of the challenge in any given area. It gives us a good visual and realistic understanding of the child's traits and challenges.

So you see, while the term 'spectrum' is heavily associated with autism, it should be used in relation to all learning styles.

It is also a very useful exercise for the students to do. We should never forget to ask the child themselves. What they experience as their greatest challenge should become a priority area for support.

7

To tell or not to tell

If you have chosen to have your child assessed and a diagnosis has been given, you then have to decide if and how you will share this information with the child. To tell a child they have a diagnosis of X or Y is a parent/guardian decision. Information of this sort should not be delivered by the teacher unless prearranged with the parent. The parent will have to predict how they will cope with this information and this will depend on the personality and maturity of the child in question. My friends will tell you that I'm fairly black and white and I'm not going to sit on the fence with this one – definitely tell the child! A big deal should not be made of it. A sensitive chat needs to be had. State the fact that they may need a little support in some areas and ask if they would be ok with that. The student needs the opportunity to express how they feel. Similarly, if the student doesn't have any specific diagnosis but the standard scores show that there is a need for intervention, then this should also be discussed with the student. We can't just suddenly start giving them support without explanation. Students have shared with me that they felt that other people must think they are stupid. With one student the difficulty was very slight, but because things weren't explained to them they thought the worst and their self-esteem plummeted.

Children know when they are not keeping up with their peers. They can react in many different fight-or-flight ways. They may act out in class in an effort to sabotage their classwork. They try to disrupt the class so that the teacher has to deal with classroom management rather than difficult academic topics. They may become the class clown to mask the fact that they simply don't understand or can't read the material, thus avoiding revealing their 'secret' to the class. On the flip side, they may become introverted and quiet, praying that the teacher won't notice their existence and therefore avoid being exposed. Unsupported learning needs affect behaviour negatively. If a student is given the reason 'why', then they can feel enormous relief. They can then feel assured that they are not the only person who has this need, and that they will be supported and therefore succeed. The proverbial line can be drawn in the sand and for many it is a chance for a fresh start.

Delivering this news needs to be done very sensitively. Try not to deliver it as some sort of bad news but rather as an answer to a puzzle. It may help to explain and justify why certain things seemed difficult. The topic should be played down a little, as to make too big a deal of it will create new anxieties. Be open and encourage your child to ask any questions they may have. You may not have all the answers there and then, but you can explain that together you can find out. Again, parental expertise reigns supreme here. If you have a good relationship with your child, then great, you can go ahead with discussing the learning difference. However, some children can get very upset, feeling that there is something 'wrong' with them. Typically, those who are closest to them often get the brunt of their emotions. If this is the way you feel it might go, then maybe ask an additional needs teacher whom they trust to deliver the news with you. I've often worked with students in this situation. Students can then ask the teacher questions, and, as they have lots of experience with other students, the teacher can assure them that they will achieve and that this is only one small element of their learning style. It is simply that – a learning style – and teachers will work with them to support their needs. The diagnosis doesn't define them.

It is at this stage that they need to be told the following:

- Lots of people in this school have a similar learning style.
- There are lots of strategies we can work on to support your learning – different programmes, assistive technology, etc.
- They could meet with older students with similar learning styles who have succeeded and achieved.
- Ask them for their opinions – what do they think could be implemented to support their learning style?

The common traits of the diagnosis can be discussed and, a bit like a sweet shop, it is often helpful for students to pick out the traits that relate to them – 'Yes, I'm a bit inflexible, but I'm not forgetful', or 'Yes, I've poor handwriting but my spelling is good' and so on. This gets them to think about their own learning style.

Making too big a deal out of the whole thing should be avoided. Again, it needs to be clear that this 'diagnosis' doesn't define the child. However, if parents keep rattling on about it, well, aren't we just proving that it is a big deal and maybe they should be worried! Think about the individual. Are they sensitive? Is softly-softly the way to go? Or are they quite clinical and able for a frank and brief discussion? You will have to let your own gut decide on this one.

8

Home–school relationships

Now be nice to each other!

Unfortunately, for far too long the parents of students with additional needs have had to fight for the rights of their children. Therefore, the default position can be one of defence and demand. Additional needs, sometimes referred to as 'special needs', were historically the domain of the charitable organisations, the saintly kind. Gone are these educational models based upon pity. The student has a right to be in class, in school. They have the right to be actively educated by the teacher!

It is essential that we assume the school you have chosen for your child or the school you teach in is inclusive unless you experience otherwise. It is a legal obligation for all teachers to teach the child in front of them. It doesn't matter what their ability or needs are. Teachers must provide a tailored experience that enables the child to experience success and progress. Teachers know this, and therefore it goes without saying. Teachers are all aware of their obligation to differentiate. There is ample training available to schools on request in the area of supporting additional needs. It is good practice for the staff of a school to have input into the areas that they need training on. If the staff feel they need support in this area then it should be arranged by school management. Failure to have an inclusive culture and practice in the school needs to be addressed, no matter what the reason. As parents we shouldn't go in all guns blazing, letting them know that you're not to be messed with, so to speak. This is a slippery path. It doesn't take copious amounts of research to tell you that a relationship of trust and respectful communication is the environment in which children thrive.

The positive environment is a three-way system – home, school and student. While you should approach the school in a positive manner, so too should you expect respectful interactions. Your child should be in an environment where they can express any difficulties safely, where they can request help. If your child doesn't communicate well in school, they should know that there is good communication between their parents and teachers, and that they can communicate any difficulties via their parents.

How to ensure good communication

Share all relevant information

Ensure you have provided all the relevant information you have on your child to the school, for example assessments and areas of difficulty. Teacher training courses and in-service training provide information on the different learning needs, the most appropriate methodologies of differentiation and accommodation within the classroom. But teachers are not telepathic: they need to know the specifics about your child. Similarly, schools should actively engage in facilitating standardised tests and observations. This information should also be shared.

Stay calm, listen and be positive

If you are unhappy with the level of provision, you are at a critical point. So many relationships have been soured at this stage. You have the right to express your discontent, and teachers have the right to explain their positions, but let's not forget that when it comes to your kids, emotions run high. Let's also not forget that teachers ... well, we just don't all take criticism very well. It is important to communicate any difficulties calmly and in a non-accusatory manner. Equally, teachers should listen to and act upon the advice from parents. If we don't listen to parents, we are not doing our job. Keeping the relationship positive is paramount.

Now I'm not saying that you need to pussyfoot around the teachers and wrap the issue up in cotton wool for fear of offending them. Some teachers need it spelt out loud and clear. However, we should also remember that in the long run the person who benefits from all parties working together is your child. I cannot tell you the amount of times I've seen students use the strained relationships between a teacher and home to manipulate a situation, i.e. get out of doing the work. 'That teacher hates me' is a comment that can't go unchecked. The relationship has to work or they can't learn. Many schools have introduced the practice of having the student also attend the parent-teacher meeting. This can work like a dream. Everyone is accountable. Students are always pleased by the amount of positive comments made by teachers who were previously accused of 'hating them'!

Be explicit – use an Individual Education Plan (IEP)

Every school will have their own procedures for devising Individual Education Plans. I would advocate that every child with a learning difference should have an Individual Education Plan. The plan should be devised after an IEP meeting with one anchor teacher, parents/guardians and the student. Other professionals such as special needs assistants or psychologists have also a lot to contribute. The plan should contain valuable information with clear targets that the student is aiming for with the support of school and home. All teachers need to be aware of the targets. The targets need to be very explicit and clearly explained so that there is no confusion. The process of an IEP meeting will ensure that the expectations of the teachers, parents and student are shared. An Individual Education Plan should not be a tick-the-box exercise. Everyone should be supporting the student, not just the Additional Needs/Special Education Teacher. When working well, it is a wonderful tool. Like most things, the process of devising the IEP is much more important than the actual A4 piece of paper created at the end. All IEPs boil down to the following:

Understanding Learning ~~Difficulties~~ Differences

- Exploring the student's strengths
- Exploring the student's challenges
- What would we like to improve? Setting clear realistic targets
- Reviewing and readjusting targets
- The IEP/Support Plan should be recorded by the school and a copy given to the parents/guardians

As mentioned above, each school will have their own policies and procedures on IEPs or support plans. The ideal is to have at least one IEP meeting a year and one follow-up meeting, depending on the needs the student. Some students will require more follow-up/review meetings. Reviewing may be constrained by time, but it is essential to review so that the achievements of the student can be celebrated and targets adjusted. The reviewing process can be done via telephone calls or video links but just make sure the student is included.

Exploring strengths and challenges

This sounds very simple and it is. Each person around the table (parent/guardian, anchor teacher, student and any other professionals involved) has to say what the student is good at. This is a very powerful part of the IEP meeting. Students gain a lot from hearing adults throw around compliments. Students can really struggle with saying what they are good at themselves. This gives an insight into the state of that student's self-esteem, which is really valuable and often ends up being a target in itself. The challenges should be delivered again in the most positive way possible. If it comes out as blunt criticism, then the whole process is counterproductive. It's usually best to let the student come up with the challenges themselves. The student must have a strong input into the whole IEP/Support Plan process. These challenges will usually coincide with yours and are much more palatable when they are self-selected. Of course, key challenges that are not seen by the student, such as blurting out answers in class, for example, are challenges that will need to be sensitively outlined.

Setting targets

Students, parents and teachers will often come up with very vague targets:

- Improve spelling
- Improve grades
- Read more
- Focus more

I'm afraid you will all have to drill a little deeper for the process to be effective, for example:

- What spelling or typing programme are they going to work on?
- How long each day will they spend on it?
- Who will help them with this?
- Who will review this with them?
- What were their results last term and by how much are they going to improve them this term?
- How will they improve them?
- What does 'study more' mean?
- How long will they study for?
- Who will they study with?

- What will they read?
- What books do they like?
- Do they have access to these books?
- Who can read with them?
- Can they retell the story they've read to someone? Who?
- Do they need a rewards system for reading a certain number of books?
- If they find they are daydreaming, what strategy are they going to use to self-regulate their focus?
- If they're blurting out in class, could they limit their questions to three per hour?

Obviously the level and depth of the targets will vary according to the student's age and ability.

It's all about balance. Targets must be achievable. It is an easy trap to have adults all agree that these are lovely targets. Everyone leaves the meeting happy and when you ask your student the next day what their targets are ... they don't know. Students should be able to tell you what their targets are and how they are going to achieve them.

Reviewing targets

Schools have finite resources and teachers are really stretched for time, but the reviewing of targets is an essential stage. If they know the teacher will forget to review them, why would they work on them? The IEP targets should be reviewed to see if there have been any improvements. Targets should be achievable within a certain timeframe. You can't be working on the same thing all year ... you'll all go mad. If you're flogging a dead horse, bury it! You can always come back to that particular target another time, maybe when the student has matured a little more. Next!

Students should be commended, acknowledged, praised and possibly rewarded for any progress or success they have achieved in relation to their targets. Sometimes when you review your targets, all parties need to be honest: 'We didn't really work on that', 'OK, let's put that one in again', 'I kinda forgot about that' ... You get the gist.

At its most basic level, the IEP is about attention. What child doesn't thrive from attention. The child can look around the table and see that everyone is there to support them.

Regular contact

It may not be possible for all students to get an IEP or support plan. The school has to prioritise and decide on which students have the greatest needs. The main thing is to make sure there is regular communication. Parents should be talking to children, teachers should be talking to children and of course parents and teachers should also have a clear and regular line of communication. Parents/guardians can always communicate clearly that they would like a meeting and have in their head the things that they and their child would like to focus on. Bono allegedly stated one time: 'I don't have a dream. I have a plan.' As a parent you can create your own mini IEP with your child at any time using the information above. Similarly, a good teacher will have targets for all their students but they should have differentiated and individualised targets for the student with learning differences. Either teacher or parent can always arrange a meeting on request or turn the regular parent–teacher meeting into an IEP meeting of sorts. If the student is involved, and strengths, challenges and targets are communicated to all parties, then you're in business.

It's worth pointing out that quite often when parents call the school to speak to a teacher, that teacher is in class teaching. Teachers are not office workers – they are not at the end of a phone. Their day is scheduled to the minute. Emails are a very effective method of contacting teachers. You can be precise and get straight to the point regarding what you need. Similarly, if you're struggling as a working parent, getting to schools for meetings can be very difficult during weekdays. Never provide too much personal information in emails and sometimes the email may just be requesting a call. Nothing is as good as a face-to-face meeting, but phone calls and emails are damn close. Not all schools provide the teacher emails so again check to see what the policy is in your school. Many schools have a policy of ringing the school secretary if you wish to get a teacher to ring you back at a time when they are not in class. Whatever the medium you use to communicate, it's communication, nonetheless.

It is important to note that you should not have to accept substandard provision. There is nothing more important than your child and they should get the very best of what is reasonably available. The keyword here being *reasonable*. As previously mentioned, schools have limits to what they can provide. It is not reasonable to demand extra resources that take away from others. Schools have to allocate their resources equitably among the children they are providing for. That being said, so many accommodations and methods of differentiation that make school a successful experience for students cost exactly nothing! Differentiation in the areas of worksheets, homework, allowing homework or assignments via email, giving extra time or simply being patient and encouraging are very reasonable accommodations and should not even need to be requested – they should be a given.

9

Homework

The cause of many an unhappy home!

It's a balancing act again. What is too much? What is a cop-out? This obviously varies according to your child's ability. Communicate with your child's school and teachers about what is considered an appropriate amount of time for them to be doing their homework. Your child shouldn't be penalised for having an additional need.

The school day is long. Consideration needs to be given to the fact that when a child has an additional need, extra focus is required for simple acts like writing, reading and concentrating on what the teacher is saying. This can be exhausting – and then we expect them to go home and do more work. The difficulty here is that the very last thing you want to do is give them a free pass, dumb it down and facilitate their underachievement. The whole process must be individualised and revisited regularly.

ASSIGN HOMEWORK CAREFULLY

Students have told me regularly that they don't like it when a teacher says, 'You only have to do 5 out of the 10 questions.' They prefer it when they are told, 'Carry on from question 2 for 15 minutes and then stop.' Another simple trap to fall into is telling them to do the first few questions and then stop. Quite often the first few questions are the easiest, so where is the challenge for them? Going over stuff they already know is a waste of time. Homework must be challenging if learning is to take place.

The point of homework is not to steal playtime from children – it is to practise a skill they are a bit wobbly at and practise it enough so that they become steady. If students are of an equal ability to their peers but have a specific difficulty, such as motor skills/handwriting, then sometimes getting them to work backwards is a good plan, thus displaying their ability to achieve the most difficult questions first.

Agree expectations of quality. Make no mistake, students with additional needs may try to wangle out of hard work, claiming that they can't do it because of their 'disability'. This is where the school and parents need to work together. The school needs to ensure that the student has an understanding of the homework before they leave the classroom. The student is responsible for alerting the teacher to the fact that they don't really understand this bit or that bit before they go home. Are they able to read the questions? So many text-books I have seen have reading ages of 17, from which homework is given to a 14-year-old with a reading age of 9. If I were an apathetic, disengaged teen, my attitude would be 'Why bother?' Parents are also responsible for rolling up their sleeves and checking what their child is doing. Parents should know if they are able to do the assigned work or if it is too difficult or taking too long. If the student is struggling, then positive but frank communication with the teacher is required. It has to be pitched at a fairly independent level. Homework completed by parents, even if the student is sitting with them, is nonetheless homework completed by parents, and therefore unhelpful for students in the long run, but we've all done it just to prevent the tears and palpitations of going into school with no homework done. If they can't do it themselves, then either there is a problem in the class, or the work is being pitched at an inappropriate level and needs to be adjusted. Homework should not be torture. Home life is precious and if homework is causing havoc, positive communication with the school needs to take place. A plan should be made to make it all a little more manageable.

10

Parenting and teaching

In this chapter my advice is more ... do as I say and not as I do!

Parenting is the greatest paradox of all time. I remember my mother-in-law coming into the maternity ward the morning after my first daughter was born. It had been a tough night – she didn't latch on and I was devastated that my copious reading of such titles as *What to Expect When You're Expecting* were not serving me well at all! I had been so smug about how prepared I was, that it made the fall to reality even longer and harder. My mother-in-law, Olive, was a stylish, gracious and elegant lady. She hugged me and congratulated me and followed it with a simple fact that has stuck with me ever since. 'Now,' she said, 'you'll worry for the rest of your life.' She was always such a positive woman, and she seemed to be condemning me to a life sentence, but boy wasn't she right!

Like most things in life, parenting is about balance. Children with learning difficulties thrive when parents are proactive and involved, but when that mothering becomes smothering ... well, the involvement is counterproductive.

I've been a special education coordinator for twenty years and have frequently worked with parents around their worries for their children. 'Accept the child you have' is the advice I would genuinely give them all. Yet, when my girls were diagnosed with dyslexia and DCD, well I suddenly felt a surge of regret for offering such bland (albeit accurate) advice.

'We'll discuss this later'

As parents we cannot help being overinvolved. When things get heated and tensions are running high it can be a useful tactic for everyone to decide to press pause and deal with the issue at a later date. Children thrive on structure and boundaries. They may think that you are too strict and controlling, but these boundaries actually make children feel safe. Deciding to 'discuss this later' allows everyone time to cool off – you will be more rational and make better decisions. The ground rules are still respected and followed through on. There are no kneejerk sanctions given that can't possibly be followed through on, like 'you can't see your friends for a month or watch telly for a month'. This is the ideal scenario of course. Believe me, to do this habitually will take some practice.

The same is true in the classroom. While students cannot get away with breaking the rules, teachers should avoid showdowns. Showdowns take up class time and some students will intentionally engage in aggravating situations so that class time can be wasted. Other students need to see that the student who breaks the rules will be dealt with but making a public exhibition is not the way to go. Often the student with additional needs gets adjusted sanctions and so open discussions in front of the class are not a good idea. Sometimes the best way for a teacher to end a difficulty is simply to put a note in their journal and move on. Parents can then read the note and contract the school if required. If you feel this is the best strategy for your child, then this can be discussed with the teacher. The student will know that they will not get away with inappropriate behaviour and that the issue will be respectively dealt with at a later stage, but not during class. It will also demonstrate to the student that the adults are working together.

Make a fresh start

One thing I learned from my own parents is that it is important for children to know that love and respect are unconditional. You might think they know this, but remember the child/teen brain is not fully developed. It is immature, and sometimes the problem lies in the fact that we are expecting mature behaviour from immature beings. Every class needs to be a fresh start. Every morning needs to be a fresh start. Grudges or prolonged silent treatments are ineffective. If you have had an issue to deal with, a fair consequence needs to be implemented, then move on, issue over.

Get involved as a parent or teacher

In relation to the child's learning difference, you will need to really get involved. As a parent you cannot just say, 'Oh, the school will deal with that.' You need to be aware of what their homework is and hence you will discover the areas they are struggling with the most. Similarly, teachers cannot say, 'Well, if they don't seem interested, what can I do.' Everyone needs to get involved! We must never accept underachievement. Establish one specific thing at a time that you will spend 10 minutes a day on together. Once that target is established, make it an adventure you are doing together.

Get your child involved

Get buy-in from your child. Ask them if there is something they would like to improve upon, rather than some defect you have spotted that you're going to force them to fix. It's a far better approach if you can possibly get them to identify something they would like to improve on. Suggest that you could help them with it for just 10 minutes a day. Nothing wrong with a little bribe or treat after a specific length of time or achievement of a certain goal.

Find the right balance

The mistake I would like to share with you is that sometimes being too regimental or militant about reaching a target can really turn a student off learning. Little and often is key. Whatever you are working on, keep it small and achievable. Overlearning (going over something again and again) can be very useful, so make sure to go over what you have done the day before or week before. Sometimes there needs to be a total break. This of course needs to be balanced with choosing an easier life of ignoring difficulties. Adopting an 'Ah it'll all work out' attitude is simply sticking your head in the sand. All children thrive from attention from their parents and teachers. So, you see where the whole balance theme will come in? Only you, who knows your child, can decide if you are pushing too hard or letting them off too lightly and therefore lowering your expectations for them. Keep it light and try to make it fun, otherwise it will all end in tears and stress – and hey presto your little angel has successfully sabotaged the whole learning experience. Patience is key!

Spend wisely

We are conditioned into thinking that the more we pay the better the product. I have met countless parents and teachers who have spent a fortune on gadgets and programmes that claim to be the best ever! Not so when it comes to learning differences. Be very cautious about spending money on different programmes. Analyse what it is your child needs help with and look at the many ways you can economically assist them. Throwing money at it is a knee-jerk reaction. Yes, assistive technology is useful but carefully examine what your child's or student's needs are before investing. We spent a lot of money on voice-to-text programmes for students who just don't like using it! Assistive technology, learning programmes, etc. have to suit the learner. So it's time to investigate the learner.

Decide what level of support is required

In the following chapters we will look at the different areas of differences and explore how you can investigate and pinpoint the exact areas where your child or student needs support. The work needs to be very individualised. Children and teens don't want to spend time working on reading, writing, etc. so for God's sake don't spend time teaching them stuff they know! Discover what they don't know and focus on that. But here is where balance comes in again. You must pitch it at a critical level of difficulty. Too easy and they're learning nothing. Too hard and they just give up. It needs to be just hard enough to feel a little uncomfortable yet achievable. I usually tell my students that it's like working out at the gym. If it's too easy, you're not getting fitter. Too hard – well, you just can't do it or you'll get hurt. So a little pain is required for progress to take place.

Avoid being overcritical

There are all sorts of personality types out there. Mistakes genuinely bother some people, but if you are that person, remember to focus more on what's right than being on high alert for what is wrong. That was the 1950s style of teaching. Over-criticism is misconstrued by sensitive personalities as failure and efforts to keep trying may be seen as pointless. Unfortunately, it seems to be an occupational hazard of so many teachers – spotting mistakes. I present a lot of work to staff and it makes me chuckle when I hear a teacher saying, 'Oh, there's a full stop needed there.' Spotting mistakes is just some people's thing!

Children cannot become too precious. They need to be resilient enough to see correction as progressive, but as adults we need to be a little less petty. By spotting mistakes are we showing off our own amazing proofreading talents? We must choose our criticism constructively. One or two points for improvement are all that is needed.

I have been blessed with two amazing young daughters. Their bouncy personalities bring me joy every day. I can't believe how lucky I am to have them in my life and I am grateful every day. It seems crazy that I would spend so much time criticising them ... and yet I do. Teachers in the past were trained to find the errors, the mistakes. Thankfully, teacher training now seems to focus on two stars and a wish: outlining two things that are really good and one thing that could be improved upon.

I can't remember where I heard the following piece of advice, if I read it or heard it ... I've no idea, but it really resonated with me and made me self-reflect:

> When your child or student walks through the door, they need to see a reaction of delight on your face. They can see in your face that you are delighted they walked in. This is a powerful message of acceptance. Now self-reflect ... how often when a child walks in are we checking their state. *Your hair isn't brushed. Wash your face. Your uniform is a mess.* These are statements of criticism. Before they walk in the next time, they will be expecting more negative and non-accepting comments. They need to know they are the light of your life. You are happy they are here and with

you. They are loved and accepted just the way they are.

I keep this concept in mind, and I wish I could be that person all of the time. I'll just have to accept that I can only be that person some of the time. When I'm pressed for time to get them to the school bus and get myself to work and my gorgeous but dishevelled daughter saunters into the kitchen, I just can't spend time on the fuzzy stuff: GET DRESSED!

11

Dyslexia

We have spoken about the dilemma of getting an assessment or not. We have spoken about the pros and cons of giving a student a diagnosis. While I will be discussing the traits and strategies for each diagnosis, remember you don't have to have a specific diagnosis to demonstrate some of the associated traits. If we take dyslexia for example, we know that there are so many people who demonstrate the traits of this learning difference. A common misconception is that dyslexic people see letters backwards or that letters jump off the page. While this may be the experience of some students, it is far too simplistic a description of dyslexia. Dyslexia shouldn't even be categorised as a disability – it is simply a style of learning. Humans *invented* reading and writing, so it doesn't come naturally. In an era where we are all about 'organic this' and 'organic that', let's remember that reading and writing are anything but organic. No two students with dyslexia display exactly the same traits. A parent may be satisfied that her child doesn't have dyslexia because they can read. Again, this is too simplistic an assumption, as the child may have developed strategies to the extent that they have overcome the difficulties. They may have put in the extra effort and time to ensure their reading is good. That doesn't mean all that extra effort isn't exhausting and therein lies the disadvantage (as opposed to disability).

The human race was designed to communicate. Communication, even among the non-verbal, is a very natural function. Babies can communicate very clearly when they demand a feed or sleep, etc. Writing and reading, however, are human-made inventions. While after some tuition it comes easily to some, those with diverse neurological wiring will struggle.

Levels of dyslexia

Dyslexia occurs on a continuum, mild to severe. A student might:

- Have mild difficulties with reading but severe difficulties with spelling
- Have severe difficulties with reading but be very organised
- Be highly disorganised and forgetful but be a good speller

The fact that no two students are the same is easy to comprehend. One characteristic of dyslexia that is confusing is that some days are more dyslexic than others. Some days students will spell and read well, other days it's a disaster. Some days they'll forget their head if it wasn't attached and it's these days that are upsetting for them and that impact severely on their self-esteem. They thought they could do these things, so why are they messing up so much today? Students with dyslexia experience self-frustration, getting so mad with themselves that they give up – what's the point?! Opting out is always an easy option.

Signs to watch out for

The student with a dyslexic brain may show dyslexic traits such as not taking to reading and spelling at the same rate as their peers, despite the fact that orally they are just as bright or even brighter. Their writing may be messy and appear careless. They may be disorganised or struggle with maths. They may have fantastic ideas. You know they get it when you are teaching them, yet the ideas never get on to a page. The main 'symptom' is that there is a mismatch between IQ tests and classroom-based tests. If a student is in the high ability range, you may presume that their school tests will result in high grades. A discrepancy between these two may alert you to a need for support. Other signs are more obvious, like a student who spells things phonetically, like 'enuf' = enough, or 'frens' = friends.

A formal assessment isn't necessary to start putting in support for the student straight away, but formal assessments may be useful for a number of reasons. A lack of progress in reading or spelling is not always due to dyslexia and the assessment may uncover some other underlying issues. If the assessment confirms dyslexia, this may come as a huge relief to students as invariably their self-esteem has been knocked when they know they are bright, but the results tell them otherwise. The most serious consequences of undiagnosed dyslexia are:

- Underachievement
- Poor self-esteem
- Habitual lack of motivation

The student has learned that they will fail, so why bother? There is a vicious cycle involved here. If reading is hard, they avoid it. If they avoid it, they will fall further behind their peers in terms of vocabulary and knowledge acquisition, so they find reading harder, so they avoid it!

Dyslexia is brain-based (neuro). It is genetic. It involves a difficulty with processing phonics. When we learn to read, we learn the sound that goes with the letter:

a = ah

Then we have to blend all these letters and sounds together to make a word:

c-a-t

Then we have a whole load of rules like:

ph = fh

The *e* at the end of a word changes the sound of the vowel:

mat and *mate*

We have to break words up to read them. How do you know where to break a word?

With dyslexia, there is no problem with seeing the letters. The difficulty lies with the process in the brain that deals with all the sounds blending together and recognising when to apply the different rules. The non-dyslexic brain will quickly recognise words they have met before without having to decode or sound out each letter and blend them together. It becomes automated. The person with dyslexia will have to labour over the phonics (or sounding out) for longer. It's frustrating and tiring, and leads to a student being slower than their peers, even when they may be far brighter.

This process of automation will happen for the student with dyslexia, but will require much more learning and relearning. Here is the paradox: the student with dyslexia needs to be exposed to a word many times before they recognise it automatically by sight (as opposed to decoding it), but if they avoid books, they won't meet the word too often.

Brain imaging has shown that students with dyslexia deal with language in a different part of the brain. When processing information takes a longer route, it slows things down and even leads to errors along the way. The brain has two sides. The left side is used to process language, reading and logic. The right side is associated with being creative and artistic. Brain imaging has shown that the dyslexic brain depends more on the right-hand side of the brain. It is not surprising, therefore, that so many people with dyslexia find success in the creative professions, such as acting and entrepreneurial business ventures.

Some teachers have reported to me that their student can read but that they don't understand a thing they have read, so how, they ask, can the student be of average intelligence? There is a good explanation for this. All that focusing on the phonics, decoding and mechanically applying all the different rules (which comes naturally to others) distracts them from what the text is actually about. Their comprehension has been hijacked by the process of decoding. It's laborious and exhausting for them!

How to help

If a student struggles with reading then the solution to this challenge truly is … reading. The more often the student reads a word, the more likely they are to recognise it again. Leave it too long and they have to go back to decoding it all over again. This is why bedtime reading with your child when they are young is so beneficial.

Many students with dyslexia have messy or poor handwriting. Their confidence gets kicked when peers comment on it or teachers criticise it without support. It's one thing to say they need to improve, but it's much better to say, 'Your handwriting needs improving and I'm going to help you.' Discuss if the spaces between words are big enough, too big or inconsistent. Making that space the same width for each word is very subjective and really difficult if you have spatial awareness difficulties. Where are they starting on the page? Sometimes students start writing in the middle of the page and don't stick naturally to the margins. They will need practice at this before it becomes automatic. Are they aligning the sentences on the lines? When their letters are different sizes, their writing can be messy. Get them to focus on same size lettering. Try to focus on the letters that go below the lines and those that go above (e.g. b, d, f, j). Discuss the optimum amount of pressure to put on the pen and on the page.

I'm not a fan of the word 'diagnosis' because it can imply an illness or something that needs a medical intervention. However, it can be beneficial to get formal assessment and early diagnosis, as early intervention is vital. With help and support the neural pathways of the brain can be physically altered and the disadvantages of dyslexia can be overcome, while still retaining the benefits of creativity. There are lots of multisensory programmes available that explicitly teach the spelling rules and word families. Repetitive teaching of rules and decoding eventually leads to the left side of the brain working more efficiently. With intensive work the student will eventually automatically recognise words. Just like when you see a person often, you recognise them.

You can learn more about reading and writing in the next chapters.

TOP TIPS FOR A DYSLEXIC STUDENT (WRITTEN FROM THE EXPERIENCE OF A 13-YEAR-OLD WITH DYSLEXIA)

'I was diagnosed with dyslexia when I was 8 and heres some top tips I've learned
1. *Its not as if you've just suddenly gotten dyslexia, it means you have had it all your life. I hate when people go on about it as if you just picked it up like it's a flew or something. Just now your diagnosed, all of those thoughts of "I am doing the same work as*

other people, and even more studying than them, oh I must not be as smart." Should be shut down. It DOESN'T mean you not as smart as other people. We just learn differently. For example I'm not good at languages, but I would be better at other things such as history, geograpy and maths. Also they say 1 in ten people have dyslexia so its not a big deal

2. Read. I know it sounds like a pain and the thoughts of "im just not a good reader, so I wont read"may come to mind , you have to practice to get good at it. But once you find a book series you love its not a chore, try going to the library and picking out some books and if you don't like them don't continue reading them. Just get a different book, but don't give up reading. its meant to be fun. Also I find that you need to really challenge yourself with books and if you cant understand words its fine as long as you are understanding the story line (if you find your cant keep up with the story and plot, try a different book) .

3. Dyslexia will always be apart of you, it's a way of thinking. But it does get a lot easier, I have found with lots and lots of reading and the help of my teachers, including extra support my scores have drastically improved. But of coarse scores aren't the be all and end all. I have mostly found that now when the teacher says "take out your english books" I now don't have the urge to scream and cry at the same time.

4. I was struggling with Irish a lot; I don't remember my scores but I do remember crying at home a lot because of it. But just remember, 1. As ive said it does get better and 2. My parents at the age of 10

agreed it was best for me to use my exemption from languages because it was causing so much stress and tears, which is great on one hand it gave me a chance to improve my english, but I often think of what would have happened if I had just stuck with it Irish. So dicuss with your parents what would be best for you .

5. What really got me is my handwriting and to this day I still get teased for by my friends for it. But since their my friends I just laugh, because we always tease each other so id say just laugh it off and don't get mad, that's the worst thing you can do.

6. you have probably have already heard this but just do your best and if you get scores you might not be happy with just say to yourself, teachers and parents "I tried my very best but I would like to improve, can I get some help? For some weird reason people are always afraid to ask for help but in my opinion its one of bravest things you can say because it means you want to improve

7. and finally don't make it too simpel, I am extremely guilty of this. I have a immensely vast vocabulary which I don't use on paper because I am either afraid of people not understanding what I write because the spelling is completely off or to be honest it takes a lot more energy and brain power than most people to get spellings right and sometimes I just don't have the energy. I am also guilty of putting ramdom letters in the middle of a long word I cant spell. Don't do this. Be proud of your work. I might have messy essays and work and it is

*not something I am proud of ,but Im putting more effort into this and I am seeing improvements
I hope this helped, from of dyslexic person to another'*

12

Reading

While we touched on reading in the last chapter, it is important to delve into this topic in a little more detail as it has important implications for the educational achievements of your child or student. If reading is a challenge then the intervention needs to be individualised and targeted. There's no point wasting time going over things the student already knows. Instead give out dictation pieces or reading pieces and discover the words they usually get wrong. Focus on these. Define which spelling pattern or word family are they associated with and explicitly teach the rules associated with that. Over-teach it and come back to it again and again until it becomes automated.

To be fair, these reading interventions can be gruelling for students. It seems like an injustice that they have to do extra work. In my experience, they need to be shown their improvements. Show them how last week they couldn't read those words and this week they've mastered those same words consistently. They made ten mistakes last week when they read that paragraph and now show them how when they were given the same piece this week, they only made three. Make the experience of success explicit and obvious. Celebrate and praise success. Little and often is key. Big long marathon runs of tuition are nothing short of torture. Some practitioners discuss the need for intrinsic motivation – the children's desire to improve coming from within. Well, maybe I'm a bad parent but I find extrinsic bribery works every time!

The basics

There are lots of lists of essential words that children need to know. There are plenty to be found free online. However, lists are very deceptive. Children can learn off lists of words to read but can they transfer their learning? Will they be able to read a learned-off word from a list when it is mixed up with hundreds of other words on a page? Only when they can recognise the word many times in a large body of text can you say they know the word.

Sometimes you need to check the basics: no matter how old the child is, if reading is a struggle for them, you need to make sure they know their basic phonics. Can they put the correct sound with each letter? I discovered with one 16-year-old that they had learned an incorrect sound for *e*. Therefore, all the words they needed to sound out that had an *e* were a struggle for them.

When the student is sure of the phonics, move on to the blends – *sn*, *pl*, *sh*, etc. There are plenty of books out there that teach the mechanics of reading. Committing to a programme is time-consuming and tiring, but absolutely worth it. Programmes that I have found useful are 'Toe by Toe' and 'Yes I Can Read'. If you start a programme, finish it. It may seem too easy and if it is, just whiz through it. You need to cover all the basics.

READING GAMES

Where possible, children should be given exercises in the form of games. For example, ask them to 'Find the word *thought* in this paragraph' or 'How many times is the word *thought* on this page?' It's all about exposure and it's all about gaining familiarity. Little and often is the key.

So many children come up with fantastic strategies to get by. It's only human to look for shortcuts. They might throw out guesses, hoping they are right, rather than spending time on decoding. Sometimes it's good to get them to read nonsense words, to check if they are decoding correctly.

The dyslexic brain loves shortcuts, so teaching word families is quite appealing. For example, 'If you learn the word *would*, what other words do you know? E.g. *Should*, *could*.'

COMPETITIONS

Some students thrive on competition but only if they feel they have a chance of winning. They may have had their self-esteem battered by the fact that their peers beat them hands down when it comes to reading. They need to engage in a new competition: one against their former self.

Ask them to read a piece of text. Count the errors and record their speed. Next, point out the errors. Go over the words. Get them to try to beat their own record. Ask them to reread and then count their errors and speed. Invariably the errors decrease and the speed increases – success! Depending on the patience of the child, you could repeat this again and again. Bizarrely, it's a fun activity. Monitor this approach as some students with anxiety may find this stressful. Remember we must always tailor to the individual.

Which books are best?

The choice of reading material is significant. It is important that the text chosen isn't too easy, otherwise the student will not be exposed to new and unfamiliar words, and they won't have a chance to practise decoding techniques. However, if the material is too difficult then it is damaging to self-esteem, confirming a negative self-belief. Giving up is inevitable and avoidance of similar unpleasant experiences in the future is guaranteed. When choosing a book, listen to them reading the first page or two. If it's too laborious, it's not for them. If they find it too easy, it's not for them. It's important that the child makes the ultimate decision guided by an adult. Explain the logic that it's important that the text is not too easy, otherwise they cannot practise properly and improve. There are lots of 'Hi-low' books out there – books with age-appropriate content but less difficult text. No tween or teen wants to read baby books. Lots of students find the thought of novels too daunting. History or science fact books are super for this type of reader. Books of short stories are good because they can reach the end quicker, feeling like they have completed the task as opposed to giving up on the big novel halfway through. Joke books can also be fun – get each member of the family to read out one joke and pass it around. Another good option is board games with cards that players have to read. It's all exposure to words.

Simple tools to make reading easier

Sometimes simply placing a piece of paper under the paragraph you want your child to read is effective, as it blocks out the rest of the text, making the task seem more manageable. Some students benefit from using a card with a window cut out of it, which they place over the text, ensuring that the student only sees one sentence at a time. This helps some students who find the text jumps out at them. Other students find black print against white pages harsh to look at. They benefit from using colour transparent overlays.

Learning environment

The right atmosphere is also important. In my experience the child who is willing to openly tell people they have a difficulty and laugh when they make a mistake gains more ground than the child who feels self-conscious or floored when someone teases them about a mispronunciation. Try to explicitly teach the child to not take themselves too seriously ... laugh off teasing about mispronunciation. Encourage your child to assertively challenge people who may have poor knowledge of dyslexia or reading difficulties. It's also very important never to ask a child to read in public without their permission. If a child refuses to read in public, this must be respected. Teachers need to be aware of this and communication from home may be necessary. However, there is always room for negotiation, for example 'If the teacher gives you the piece the night before and goes over it with you before you read it, will you have a go at reading even three lines tomorrow?'

Visits to libraries and bookshops create an excitement around books. Let's face it, children are materialistic – books are possessions, things to be had. So if they want a book, get it. The library is now a fun and vibrant place with the most up-to-date books. There are now books to suit everyone. The books are interesting and diverse. The staff are more than willing to source anything you may need.

Paired reading

Paired reading is tried and tested. I'd never spend too long at this with any student but it is very effective. Here's how it works. You both read the passage aloud together. You demonstrate the speed and intonation, acting as a scaffold and a support to the student. They can just mumble the words they don't know as you will be there to say these words. You can start off loud and then fade away, letting the confident reader drown you out. Eventually you may decide to let them read themselves aloud and you act only when they hesitate, to prompt and encourage them to break up a difficult word. If they stall at a difficult word, try to get them to work it out. Get them to look at the beginning and the end of the word. Let them guess the word and only then, if they really need it, tell them the word and move on. This also gives you, as the significant adult, an awareness of where they are really at with their reading and where they need help.

Your approach

When a child is reading, you must examine your own personality traits. If you're a perfectionist, try to remember that this is about building the child's self-confidence. If they make lots of errors, then the piece may be too difficult for them, but try not to over-correct. The days of the over-strict school/parent are over. It's well established that children thrive where they feel safe to make mistakes, free from excessive reprimands, in an environment full of encouraging phrases such as, 'You're doing great', 'Keep going ... you're making great progress', 'You couldn't do that yesterday and today you can.' We are never looking for perfection – we are thrilled with improvement no matter how small the steps ... forward is forward.

Comprehension

Of course, with all this focus on the mechanics of reading and decoding, it's essential that the main purpose of reading isn't lost – comprehension. The only function of reading is to learn something from it, be it a factual point or a plot in the novel or a description of a character. While pair reading, for example, it's good to take a pause and ask questions about the text. 'How do you think he felt when she said that?', 'That was a bit mean, don't you think?' Or 'What do you think will happen next? Bet you she will do X.' Get a discussion going and you'll be able to see if they are simply decoding words or actually reading. If they know you are going to engage them in discussion, they will be more focused. This goes for reading schoolwork as well. Reading the questions at the end of the chapter before they start reading the chapter itself is always good for getting them to read for meaning. A pre-reading exercise like turning the headings into questions is also a good way to get them to read for comprehension.

Enjoy reading!

Remind your child that reading is an enjoyable pastime – something they can enjoy whenever they are bored. The best way to demonstrate this is to be a role model. Try to read for pleasure yourself so that they can see first-hand that reading is a leisure activity.

Reading supports

While it's important to never give up on the acquisition of reading skills, the child's academic progress must not be sabotaged because they are spending all their time on reading. There are lots of reading supports out there that children can avail of. Almost every topic in the world, once Googled, has an appropriate video online that can explain it. Parents and teachers must be cautious as regards ensuring online material is age-appropriate but these are invaluable methods of acquiring knowledge without the labour of reading. If the student is doing a project on volcanoes when you look up Google Videos or YouTube, you will find videos suitable for five-year-olds right up to postgraduate university level. If you want to support your student or child, you could do the leg work for them. You could take the topic and sieve through the videos to find the most appropriate ones. Be specific about your search. If it's a video to explain volcanoes to a fourteen-year-old, then put 'explaining volcanos for teens' into your search. There are numerous apps and software packages that can read textbooks to the student so that they can acquire the necessary knowledge. Apps change and update frequently, so it is best to link with the additional needs coordinator or psychologist to see which one they find best given the student/child's age.

13

Spelling and handwriting

My advice to my students now is: never let poor spelling get in the way of writing down a good idea.

All too often I have seen students with beautiful extended vocabulary dumb down their writing. Choosing small babyish words simply because they are unsure of their spelling, as opposed to using the colourful and expressive language that is required to communicate images and passion about certain topics, or explaining facts with in-depth displays of knowledge using extravagant terminology – you know, using writing for what it was created for!

Naturally as educationalists we should always try to improve a child's spelling, but school isn't a 'spelling' institution. Focus on knowledge 99 per cent of the time and on spelling for the remaining 1 per cent. A delicate student will be floored by too much criticism of their spelling, leading them to feel they are no good at the subject itself. Students need to be confident enough to say, 'Yes, I'll focus on one or two spellings in that piece, but what did you think of the content?' Teachers should be aware that marking more than four spellings to be worked on in any given piece of work is poor practice.

I mentioned before that I was blessed with teachers who gave me positive support. I suggested leaving an Honours English class in sixth year because I was aware of my spelling weaknesses. I was quickly told, 'Don't be daft ... sit back down!' Grand, permission to stay, I wasn't a fraud just bluffing my way through. Had I had an older-style teacher who believed that spelling was in some way linked to intelligence, I would have been snookered and hence underachieved.

Another teacher explained to me that she believed spelling was like music – you either have an ear for it or you don't. I loved this explanation – no one gets distressed if you aren't good at music, so why should spelling be any different? She went a step further. It's one thing to say don't worry too much about it, but it's another to say it's not the end of the world but you don't need to just accept it either. There is always room for self-improvement. She gave me three commonly misspelt words each day to focus on. Teachers' and parents' attitudes are critical. Be supportive and encouraging yet challenging and consistent. It's tricky to balance a sufficient level of standards and expectations with being too militant or setting amounts that are overloading and stressful. There are no set guidelines for this. You will have to individualise, but make sure you start off with the little and often approach.

The basics in supporting spelling

Be reassuring

Reassure students that you know that what they are saying in their writing is more important than their spelling.

Accommodation

Here's a question to ask their teacher. In general, do they deduct marks for poor spellings and grammar? As a general guide, if a student is making more than eight spelling mistakes in every one hundred words they are *likely* to be entitled to a spelling and grammar waiver. We should support students in improving spellings, but nothing is to be achieved by having a page full of corrections. Teachers should let students know that they will mark a few spellings that they can work on. Explicitly tell the student not to worry too much about spellings when writing down their information, ideas or opinions as they will not be taking off marks for poor spelling or grammar. This is an arrangement just for them and not for the whole class and that they do however expect them to do their best. For older students where teachers are unsure if they will be getting a spelling and grammar waiver in their state exams, I would recommend they give the grade with the waiver and without.

Personalise spellings

Get students to think of the words they always mix up and concentrate on learning these. Advise them to have a notebook to hand when they are writing, so that when they come across a word they aren't sure of, they can jot it down (misspelt as it may be) to either look up later or work on with an adult.

There are lots of lists on the internet, such as the 100 most used words in the English language. I have found it useful to make up paragraphs with these words laced through the text. The paragraphs can be made more appealing if they are on topics that you know interest the student. I then dictate these paragraphs to the student. From this I will be able to see exactly which spellings the student finds challenging. Focus on the fact that they may have got the beginning of the spelling right and only went wrong with the last two letters. So often adults just wipe out a whole word as being misspelt. This is not the case. They will usually have most of it right and this needs to be celebrated. It makes the task of learning this spelling much less daunting if they know they are almost there already. Pop two or three of these words into their personalised notebook to be worked on over the coming week. Advise them to use these words in their writing whenever they get the opportunity.

Spelling families

As we discussed in the section on reading, there are word families in spelling. Highlight to the student that if they can spell *rain*, they can easily spell *train*, *strain*, etc.

Repetition

Revisit the spellings they have learned on a regular basis. This embeds them into their memory, and when they get them consistently right, you can emphasise this solid and visible success. Voila – self-esteem energy boost! Children and teens with a learning difficulty can be so sensitive that they tend to catastrophise: 'I can't do it', 'There's no point', 'I'm useless.' This means that when success is achieved, it must be explicitly pointed out and celebrated.

Spelling rules

As teachers and parents/guardians we should check with the additional needs team in the school to discuss the spelling programmes the school uses. Settle on one programme and work on this both in school and at home. There are lots of spelling rules that the student with a learning difficulty will have to overlearn or repeat learn. So many parents are surprised by the rules of spelling that they themselves have just picked up along the way and which they don't even have to think about. The student with spelling difficulties needs to learn these rules explicitly, but only one or two at a time. No one wants to be overwhelmed and upset, otherwise it all goes to pot! Keep at it until you're finished rather than stopping and starting. Again, the little and often rule applies. 'Look, say, cover, write, check' is a tried and tested method that can be used. Remember, however, that lists are no good unless a student can use it in a piece of text and slot this spelling into their writing when appropriate in different contexts.

Visuals

When you are working on a spelling, get the student to use different colours for different parts of the spelling.

This may appeal to the visual learner. Some students really like getting a visual (e.g. from Google Images) to go with the new spelling.

Spelling dissection

Inspecting the spelling of words with the student is always worthwhile. Discuss the beginning of the word and the end. Is there a word within the word? It's like examining a person – are their ears big or is their nose small? The more they intensely examine a word, the more familiar they become with it, and the more likely they are to be able to not only spell it but read it when they meet it again.

Proofreading

PUKE! Who wants to proofread? It's not fun but 'it needs to be done' is the mantra that should be employed. Advise the student to read what they've written out loud (whisper reading) – this is the most effective way for them to spot errors. Sometimes students will not have spelling errors per se, but they may have written double words such as 'of of' or they might omit words. The brain tends to insert words that it thinks should be there, rather than what's actually written down. They'll miss these errors if they just glance back over their work, but when they read their sentences out loud, they'll realise that it doesn't sound right. It's better for them to spot their own errors than have someone else criticising their work. When they correct their own work, they'll get a feeling of being a bit of a perfectionist as opposed to someone else spotting their errors making them feel like a failure. Getting students to go back over their work is frequently met with resistance and comes with a health warning for parents!

Check for speech and language difficulties

If spelling difficulties persist, it may be worth checking if the student has a speech and language difficulty. If they are mispronouncing a word, this may influence how they sound it out and spell it. As I mentioned earlier, getting their sight and hearing tested is good practice if they have a learning difficulty, as spelling words incorrectly may be influenced by poor hearing.

Handwriting is like basket weaving!

I firmly believe that everyone should learn the mechanics of writing. However, I also firmly believe that in the not-too-distant future we will all be using technology to write and communicate all of the time and handwriting will become somewhat of an artisan skill. Handwriting can become a shameful experience for students. Handwriting is strongly connected with sensory processing and for some students, no matter how hard they try, their writing can be very messy and sometimes almost illegible.

Spacing and pressure

Link with the additional needs team in your school to see what handwriting programmes they use and recommend. Children should actively try to improve their handwriting. One thing that can be focused on is the width required for spaces between words. Making that space the same width between each word is very subjective and really difficult if you have spatial awareness difficulties, vestibular difficulties or proprioceptive difficulties. The vestibular system is a sensory system in the inner ear that impacts on a student's coordination and movement. The proprioceptive system is located in our muscles and joints allowing us to know the correct amount of pressure or body position required to carry out a task such as writing. Writing requires consistency in spaces. When the letters are of different sizes, handwriting can look messy. Good handwriting requires the student to put an optimum amount of pressure on the pen and on the page.

Avoid too much focus on handwriting

Just like with reading, students with spelling or writing difficulties should always strive to improve, but ultimately it's about the student achieving academically or in work or socially (their ability to communicate in emails, letters, etc.). Too much focus on handwriting comes at the cost of being a slow writer. Beautiful handwriting cannot come at the cost of getting knowledge down onto the page.

Accommodations and support

While we can help students to work on their handwriting, consideration needs to be given to the list of accommodations that can make their life easier when it comes to handwriting, for example:

- *Handouts*: Do students really need to copy a load of work down off a board? Teachers can provide handouts or email notes and presentations to them.
- *Photographs*: Allow the student to take a photo of the board to avoid having to take things down.
- *Spellchecker*: Allow the student to use their laptop or tablet with a spellchecker.
- *Word processor*: Typing their work.
- *Voice to text*: Using voice-to-text technology bypasses the need for the mechanics of handwriting.
- *Text to speech*: Using the text-to-speech function on devices will allow the student to hear their mistakes when playing it back.

There is always the debate about introducing an accommodation that they may not be entitled to when they reach the upper end of their school years. There is nothing to stop you introducing some of the accommodations mentioned above on a partial basis just to make school life flow a little easier. We are not necessarily making them dependent on an accommodation such as voice-to-text; it is really about ensuring they are given the opportunity to keep up with their peers. When the student gets to more senior years you need to link with the school's additional needs team or psychologist to investigate which accommodations they will be entitled to. This can also be investigated at *examinations.ie* under the section of schools and reasonable accommodation. These strategies need to be practiced. There is one thing applying for the use of a word processor because it is their entitlement but if their typing skills are poor it may actually slow them down. Accommodations are also discussed in detail in Chapter 3.

Allow time

Is the student's handwriting speed a difficulty? Is giving them extra time during class or for homework be an option? Would rest breaks help?

Typing and voice to text

It might help the student if they learned how to type. This is fantastic for the student whose handwriting is illegible. It also has advantages for the student whose handwriting is very slow. However, some students with severe fine motor difficulties may also find typing a struggle and so they should consider voice-to-text functions on their devices instead. If they are using voice-to-text technology, the student will need to practice speaking very clearly and making each word distinct. Your laptop or tablet will not be able to decipher the words if your words run into each other. Voice to text may not be an option if there is a coexisting speech and language difficulty.

14

Dysgraphia

Students with dysgraphia have a specific difficulty in expressing their thoughts in written form. When you read the chapter about DCD/dyspraxia and the chapter relating to difficulties with spelling, you will see huge similarities between the difficulties involved. Poor handwriting is the main indicator for dysgraphia, but how will you know if it's dyspraxia or dysgraphia or dyslexia? My advice is to have less focus on the label and more focus on what the difficulty is. Poor handwriting is a difficulty with all three labels. Therefore, many of the strategies that are discussed in the chapters on DCD, spelling and dyslexia should be cross-referenced here. Students with dysgraphia have a difficulty with spelling in common with students with dyslexia. However, one major difference is that quite often students with dyslexia have a difficulty with reading. This is not the case for dysgraphia.

A psychologist or occupational therapist can diagnose dysgraphia, but no matter what the outcome of any report, if a student's verbal ability far surpasses their written ability, an intervention is required. A word of warning, however, is that many students with dysgraphia have lovely handwriting. You need to monitor if they are working so hard on having nice writing that they lose track of the content, or if handwriting takes up an extraordinary amount of time so that they never seem to be able to finish their work in the allocated time.

It is so important that students are not reprimanded for being lazy or not trying hard enough. High expectations should be set for children in line with their peers, as dysgraphia has no impact on their ability or intelligence.

Signs to watch out for

The student's mechanics of writing may be a tell-tale sign:

- An awkward pencil grip
- Pressing too hard on the pencil
- Inconsistency with letter shapes
- Inconsistency in the direction of letters
- Misjudging where the letters are on the line

Children with dysgraphia often prefer to write in print rather than cursive as they feel it is more legible. It may be more legible but it is far more laborious, and the mechanics of writing distracts them from their thought process and their ability to express their thoughts.

How to help

For younger children, support their learning of letter formation in a very tactile way, tracing sandpaper letters, or writing letters in the sand. Spend time on building up their fine motor skill strength by doing exercises such as pinching pegs out of clay or making chains out of beads. As the child gets older, repetition of letter formation via tracing will build up their muscle memory to make the letter formation more automatic. Some students find using graph paper useful to help them determine size and letter spacing.

Teaching proper pencil grip early is very useful as it is hard to unlearn a poor habit. Link with the school about the different pencil grips out there. Watch a YouTube video on how to correctly grip a pencil with your child and get them to try it out. Have fun in deciding which pencil grip they feel is comfortable. The key then is to stick with it and practise it a lot. Link with the school to see which handwriting programmes they like to use. All students have to learn how to write, but a student with dysgraphia just needs to spend more time completing as many of these programmes as is tolerable. Tolerable is an important word here. Short and often is essential, otherwise you will just turn the child right off and no progress can be made in such a scenario.

Older students

As the student gets older they will devise their own strategies and mechanics of writing. You can only spend so long supporting this. As they get older, education is about knowledge. Their exam results are all about their ability to impart and demonstrate their amazing knowledge to the person correcting their work. No one gets into college or an apprenticeship or a job because they have fabulous handwriting. If an examiner can read their writing, then it is good enough!

Remember that we said a student's difficulties with the mechanics of their writing interferes with their thought process. One way to avoid this knowledge disappearing before it reaches the page is to say it out loud first. A student can form their idea verbally or dictate their answers first and then write them down.

Accommodations

Students with dysgraphia may be allowed to type their answers and thus mitigate their difficulties in writing. Some will be allowed to use speech-to-text software where they can verbally give their answers and the software will transcribe it. Even if students do not qualify for such accommodations, they should be practised on a partial basis by students with writing difficulties as they will allow students to get through their schoolwork with greater ease. Using voice-to-text software takes a bit of practice, as does typing, so if the student is permitted to type or use voice to text, they will be of little use to them if they have not practised using them.

15

Dyscalculia

'I was no good at maths either' is one of the worst things a teacher or parent can say to their child – even if it's true. It's simply giving them permission to say, 'Ah sure, I won't bother.' Dyscalculia is often referred to as being dyslexic in the area of maths. Similar to the approach for dyslexia, the main thing to remember is that having dyscalculia is not a reflection of a student's intelligence. As with dyslexia they can be tested to see if they have dyscalculia, but regardless of a diagnosis or not, if a student is having difficulties with maths, they need targeted interventions.

If a student has a mild general learning difficulty, their difficulty with maths may be related to a poor working memory or processing speed. Sometimes a student may be having real difficulties with maths simply because in their formative years they had a gap in learning or suffered a trauma that interrupted them acquiring some very important simple but foundational concepts and therefore were moved on to complex and abstract concepts without this foundation.

Maths anxiety

Perhaps the student is having difficulties with maths because they have what can be regarded as 'maths anxiety'. They may have struggled with one element of maths and in their head they made a fool of themselves in front of their peers. They may have gotten everything wrong on one particular day, and the repercussions of that experience have stayed with them whenever they study maths. They become paralysed with fear and therefore cannot master the content being taught. Fear interrupts concentration and focus, two skills essential when studying mathematical concepts.

Like all subjects, maths consists of numerous topics. There are many different elements to it, including:

- Arithmetic – adding, subtracting, multiplication and division
- Algebra – using symbols (e.g. X = 3, so what is 2X?)
- Geometry and trigonometry – shapes, lines and angles

A student can be totally at a loss with one maths topic and be fantastic at another. So when a student says, 'I'm no good at maths', you need to find the bit they can do and demonstrate to them that they may find one particular topic difficult, but not this topic.

Getting past the maths anxiety is essential as a first step. Students who have been traumatised by some experience of mathematical failure need to experience success. Their confidence needs to be built up and the anxiety dissipated before any learning can take place.

Getting past maths anxiety

If a student believes they are no good at something and that they are unlikely to get better at it, then they may not waste their time trying or allow themselves the vulnerability of definite failure. If you were asked to compete in a weight-lifting event, you are likely to refuse – you'll get hurt and make a show of yourself because you just can't do it. If it is clear that there is some challenge around maths for the student, try focusing back on the basics. Once you have gone over some foundations see if there is any difference in their progress thereafter. It may be that one short intensive course on the basics brings their abilities up to their peers. Perhaps it gives them the confidence to rid themselves of the anxiety that preoccupied their mind and prevented effective concentration.

Signs to watch out for

The following are signs that a student may have a maths difficulty:

- Relies on counting on their fingers as they get older
- Can't explain how they got an answer
- Mixes up signs
- Cannot line up figures correctly
- Struggles with estimations
- Can do a maths task one day but can't transfer the skill to a different question

Dyscalculia

- Gets overwhelmed and confused
- Mixes up numbers, e.g. 24 and 42
- Struggles with copying down numbers
- May struggle in telling the time
- Tries to learn things off to just get by that day, rather than understanding how to do something
- May need extra 'wait time' to allow the processing of the maths problem to take place

How to help

Going back to basics

Like every other learning difficulty, you have to discover what the student doesn't know. So what are the basics you need to check?

Counting and the number system

- Can the student count correctly? Are they leaving any numbers out? Can they count backwards? Can they add on two, go back five? Can they count in multiples of 2s or 5s or 10s?
- Do they understand 10s, 100s, 1000s? Can they tell you what the 3 means in 3, 32, 302, and 3,004?
- Do they understand that numbers are composed of other numbers, e.g. 8 = 2+6 or 4+4?
- Do they know that 10 can be broken into 1+9 or 8+2 or 7+3, and so on?
- Do they know that between 1 and 2 there are ten points? Or that halfway is 1.5? Is 1.8 closer to 1 or 2?
- Are they lining up the sum correctly, e.g. with the 10s under the 10s and the units under the units?

Estimations and comparisons

- Looking at pictures of jars, can they say which is half full or which jar is fuller?
- Can they put random numbers in numerical order?
- Can they find pages of a book using the index for a particular topic?
- Can they correctly play guess the number? They pick a number in their head and others ask, 'Is it bigger than X?', 'Is it smaller than Y?' They can only answer yes or no.
- Do they have a visual or spatial perception difficulty? Can they pick out two jars that look about equal? Can they distinguish which side of an object is longer?
- Do they confuse numbers, e.g. 9s and 6s?

Maths facts/operations/symbols

- Do they know their tables? This may require over-learning and repetition in junior years. If tables still present as a difficulty into their teens even after intensive work, then it can come as a great relief when adults suggest parking tables and rely more on the calculator.
- Is their maths difficulty a physical one? (Using a ruler and moving it around requires good fine motor skills and even more advanced motor skills when they move on to using a compass and protractor.)
- Can they read the text? Sometimes the maths question that they can easily do is hidden in a blob of text they can't read.

Getting students to think and explain out loud *how* they did something or *why* they did it may uncover some basic skills that have been learned incorrectly. They will need to be unlearned and relearned. Now that's not easy, but it's better to know than not to know.

Making the neurons connect with confidence

I often hear a teacher say that a student understood a concept on Monday but on Tuesday they couldn't. If a student has acquired a new skill, it needs to be drilled and practiced, but also we need to ensure they are not just copying a sequence of steps. Remember, students with dyscalculia do not have an IQ difficulty and they will find strategies to 'get them through'. It is not enough for the student to remember a sequence of steps: they must be able to apply the skill in a problem that is presented in a slightly different format. All too often, students with dyscalculia are not given this consolidation time – they are quickly shuffled on to the next chapter in order to keep up with the class. It's a real catch-22 situation: we don't want them to fall behind so we fast-track them through, but if they are not afforded the opportunity to consolidate and practice the skill, they lose the permanent ability to apply it, and it's all been for nothing. When they revisit the topic again, they can't do it and feel stupid, proving in their own heads 'I'm no good at maths.' To *nearly* have a skill isn't enough. They shouldn't move on until they are confident they know it.

On the flip side, drilling a skill where there just doesn't seem to be any progress is a form of torture in itself! As mentioned above, if they have drilled their tables for years and they still don't know them, get a calculator and move on. Move on to a topic they can master, so that they can reclaim their sense of self-belief.

Watch your reactions!

We parents are the worst at concealing sheer shock at the fact that our child spent an hour on a topic yesterday and definitely knew it, but today they look at us blankly, like we've just asked them to recite a poem in Russian. Even if we don't blurt out something insensitive like, 'How in the name of God do you not know that after all the time we spent on it yesterday?', your face might say it all. Teachers also need to work on their poker face. If a student doesn't know it, then remember you are dealing with a learning 'difficulty'. If they knew it, then they wouldn't have a learning difference and you wouldn't be reading this book! It's essential that you are understanding and reassuring that it's perfectly normal to forget things. Quickly revert to a question or element of the problem you know they can do – end in success and their confidence will be kept intact.

Scaffolding

Like reading or any other skill in life there are a number of steps:

1. Model, i.e. demonstrate how it's done
2. Get the student to do it with you, then move on to the next step
3. Do it together but let them do sections on their own
4. Allow the student to do a larger section or longer sum independently and only help if they are stuck
5. Allow them to do it independently

It's just like teaching someone to ride a bike. However, you must start at a level they are confident with. You must make sure they have the foundations mentioned above. The ideal learning environment is when it is hard enough to be a slight struggle. Too easy and nothing is learned. Too hard and it damages confidence. The math skill needs to be at just the right level of difficulty in order to challenge and progress the student.

Maths language

Sometimes when difficulties with maths are investigated you will find that the root of the difficulty lies with a language difficulty. When students hear or read a 'problem' to be solved, it is bound up in words that send them into a maze. I gave the following problem to a thirteen-year-old: *A group of students carried out a survey outside a shop for two hours. Illustrate their findings in a bar graph.* I got him to highlight the words he didn't understand. He highlighted 'survey' and 'illustrate'. Without these two words the problem doesn't make sense. Lots of students with dyslexia will struggle with reading and therefore have difficulty figuring out what is being asked. Similarly, a student with a language difficulty will find listening to the teacher's use of words to explain the method very confusing and even overwhelming. Students learn best in maths when they are actively engaged with the problem solver, asking the teacher or parent why they did this or that. Students with speech and language difficulties may find it difficult to explain or verbalise what it is they do not understand and therefore just opt out of asking for the clarification essential to understanding the method. In this scenario it may be wise to observe the student carry out each step in solving a problem and you may be able to see where they are challenged rather than getting them to verbalise it.

Parents teach maths far better than maths teachers

For students who have difficulties with maths, the key to success is working with concrete examples that they can clearly see the relevance of in life. I've often heard students in class say, 'Why do I need to know this?' It is a worthwhile exercise for tweens and teens to work out how much they need to earn in order to live a comfortable life or how to work out tax or budgeting for holidays.

Parents can take every opportunity in life to teach maths:

- 'This costs €16. What change will I get if I pay with a €20 note?'
- 'The recipe is for four people. I'm going to double the recipe. How many eggs will I need?'
- 'Do you think that chest of drawers will fit in your room? Here's a measuring tape … will you check?'

There needs to be real-life, tactile and visual interaction with maths. Give lots and lots of opportunities for guessing (estimation). Make it fun:

- 'How many millilitres are left in that bottle do you think?' Get everyone to guess and then measure it.
- Have a grow wall in your home. Measure the differences in the height of family members in a year. Work out the height differences between siblings.
- Enjoy doing puzzles and Lego together.

- Get your child to keep the score in games, be the banker or move the markers after the dice is rolled.

Teaching a maths skill to a student with difficulties sometimes requires one-to-one help. This just isn't possible in all school settings. However, as a parent if you can figure out what skill your child definitely needs work on, you can help them to practise and acquire that skill and give them that one-to-one help they need. You don't have to know everything on the curriculum. Take it bit by bit, step by step – forward is forward.

Working memory difficulties

When working with maths, students often have to hold a small piece of information in their heads before they move on to the next section. This is exactly what working memory is. If they have a weakness in the short-term mental storage of information, then maths will be difficult for them. Students with a mild general learning difficulty will need support in this regard. Start at a point of success and practise skills in small steps. There is no rush. Progress is progress. Rushing causes such anxiety and is so counterproductive. It is far better to learn a little bit, well and slowly, than to learn nothing really fast.

16

Down's syndrome

Down's syndrome is a genetic condition caused by the presence of an extra chromosome, and while people with Down's syndrome may have similar physical characteristics, let this not fool you into thinking that any two students with Down's syndrome are in any way similar.

Like every other topic we have discussed, it is important to get some baseline information on the individual. If you are a teacher, concentrate on spending time gathering information from the student's parents, previous teacher(s) and, most importantly, from the student themselves. Find out what they like to do and are good at. Are they good readers, singers, writers? Find out their passions – food or animals or music. Find out where they are at in terms of their functional life skills. Can they read a timetable, pack a lunch, make a phone call? Celebrate the student's skills and abilities and then after consultation with the student, parent/

guardian and additional needs team, decide what is it you want them to learn and how you will all go about it.

So often we strive to get our child to do state examinations. The intention is good. We want them to have goals and achieve. Be careful we are not enrolling them in stressful programmes so we can feel a sense of achievement as educators or parents. Similarly, it is vital we do not underestimate the student's abilities. Opting them out of anything challenging denies them the progression they are well capable of. Striking the correct point of challenge requires observation and consultation.

It is my experience that when teaching students with Down's syndrome you need to be very clear with your directions, making sure you have eye contact and engagement when you are giving instructions. Keep all discussions concise. Consequences need to be instant. If you are giving praise for a piece of work they have completed, it is best to give it straight away. Similarly, correcting a student for yesterday's misbehaviour is a waste of time and confusing for them.

When setting work for students with Down's syndrome, be mindful of the fact that they may have other health challenges such as heart difficulties or hearing difficulties.

Many students I have worked with are very visual and learn best through concrete examples and visuals. Learning through music is always a winner and some teachers are more skilled at this than others. Be careful to have a clear and consistent environment. It can be very confusing for students if they are allowed to be giddy in one class and then have to instantly swap to silently sitting at a desk doing written work 10 minutes later. Make sure to allow for processing time when you give an instruction and only give one instruction or piece of information at a time. Most of the strategies discussed in the chapter on general learning difficulties are very relevant here. The student with Down's syndrome may have learning difficulties ranging from mild to profound, and like all learning differences discussed, every individual is different.

Once you have decided on the goals, make sure they are achievable in bite-size steps that can be celebrated along the way. All students with Down's syndrome progress at their own pace. So what if it takes a little longer, as long as you get there.

17

General learning difficulties

We hear a lot about specific learning difficulties such as dyslexia or dyscalculia. They are specific to spelling, reading or maths. A general learning difficulty (GLD) is a learning difficulty in numerous areas. All students with a general learning difficulty progress and acquire skills throughout their lives just like anyone else – it is usually just at a slower pace. In the section on assessment jargon above I spoke about GAI or General Ability Index. If a student's GAI score is significantly below average, then they would be regarded as having a general learning difficulty.

Categories of general learning difficulties

To get a diagnosis of a general learning difficulty, students will undertake an assessment with a professional. A general full-scale IQ test will be administered. The professional may use these tests to arrive at a point on the General Ability Index or GAI. There are lots of subsections to these ability tests. Students will have strengths in some areas and may be really challenged in others. The average is calculated across all the subsections and the standard scores will determine if the student fall into the category of having a GLD. If their score falls at around 100, they are regarded as being in the average range. Falling below 85 is where targeted interventions may be required.

The learning difficulties can be categorised as:

- Borderline mild general learning difficulty   70–80
- Mild general learning difficulty (MGLD)   50–69
- Moderate general learning difficulty   35–49
- Severe general learning difficulty   20–34
- Profound learning difficulty   <20

GAI or IQ scores cannot measure a student's resilience ability, kindness, humour or the amount of joy they bring to others. So with a diagnosis of GLD, remember that this is a score that only makes a prediction based on information at that moment in time. Students take spurts of progression so not all predictions are accurate. The scores enable us to see that a different pace of learning is required, but learning *will* take place and skills *will* be acquired. I have seen many students with a GLD achieve wonderful success. This success should not come at a cost. Yes, we want all students to achieve their potential, but it should not mean the student burns the candle at both ends just to prove they can get the same grades as their peers. A student's emotional health is far more important than any academic result. If they can reach a balance of working hard with support without undue stress, then the results are always so rewarding for the student.

Borderline MGLD or MGLD

The regular pace of work in the classroom may prove to be a significant challenge to the student. They may feel overwhelmed, get upset or give up unless teachers are aware and provide tailored, differentiated work. Students with a GLD tend to learn best with concrete and tangible examples. As the curriculum progresses, tasks become more abstract and less concrete. Reduced vocabulary may also add to difficulties. Reading, writing, spelling and maths will be at a slower pace, and therefore all the strategies for the difficulties already discussed in previous chapters are relevant here too. Overlearning is key. Repetition, praise, repetition, praise. It is important not to torture our children! Little and often is an effective policy. Downright determination and patience on the part of the student, teachers and parents are the key to success here.

How to help

ORCHESTRATE SUCCESS

Reinforce the student's confidence so that this success can be built upon. These are a very delicate group of students. Their experience of the classroom needs to be a safe and encouraging one in order for real progress to be made. The child with a GLD needs concrete evidence of their progress, e.g. 'Last week you couldn't do X, Y or Z. Today you can do X and Y and we are going to keep going with Z.' Give a certificate of achievements for each goal, rather than general wishy-washy praise.

HAND-OVER-HAND AND SCAFFOLDING STRATEGIES

Hand-over-hand and scaffolding strategies are effective. When a student has a whole load of words coming at them that they don't understand, it simply becomes white noise. If you are teaching your child a new skill, for example rinsing, making a sandwich or using a ruler to draw a box, you must:

- Demonstrate it for them
- Carry out the task hand-over-hand a few times – get them to have their hands over yours so they can feel how it's done
- Let them do a little of the task on their own, but if they struggle, go back to hand-over-hand for a few times
- Get them to do it themselves under observation, giving encouraging comments and guidance
- Give them lots of opportunities to do the task independently, giving lots of praise

EMOTIONAL SUPPORT AND VIGILANCE

Children with a borderline MGLD or MGLD may mature at a slower pace than their peers and as a consequence feel happier and more secure with children who are younger than they are. The slower pace of social maturation will become more obvious during the teen years and this can be a difficult time. Emotional support is so important. Their immaturity may make them vulnerable, so keep a keen eye on the peers they are mixing with. Extra vigilance is needed to monitor their phone and web use. Helping them to see what a good friend is, as opposed to a bad one, is a far more valuable lesson than, say, algebra.

Students may struggle with understanding conversations their peers are having. Their peers' conversations may contain abstract ideas or vocabulary they don't yet possess. They may feel lost. Their conversations may be out of context and appear immature when they do join in. Perhaps their formulation and expression of ideas are not fully developed as yet. When a child is holding their own with their peers or in school, it needs to be acknowledged that this may be due to the immense effort and determination of that child. This can be downright exhausting and sometimes emotionally upsetting. More often than not, children with MGLD/GLD are social butterflies and can hold their own with their peers and maintain genuine friendships. We need to acknowledge that we cannot fit everyone into a pigeonhole. It's necessary to be a little more cautious and keep a watchful eye as they develop their independence.

Moderate learning difficulties

These students will have learning and social differences similar to those mentioned above, but at a more intense level. They will have reached their milestones at a delayed rate. But remember this is not a race. The developmental milestones are indicators of moderate learning difficulties, but the important thing is to celebrate the milestones when they come.

How to help

TAILORED CURRICULUM

It is likely that academic work will need to be reduced or modified significantly. This is very dependent on the individual student. We have students who follow a tailored curriculum and enjoy the learning process. Others take the same exams as their peers but with a reduced number of subjects. Teachers and parents need to work together to find the right point of challenge for the student. You need to find a challenging level without inflicting stress. Students cannot be set up for failure. If we know they are likely to fail at a topic, why would we subject them to failure, just because it's on the curriculum? On the other hand, they need opportunities to demonstrate what they can do. Students will always surprise you with their ability. To pitch the level too low is depriving them of the opportunity to advance.

ORCHESTRATE SUCCESS

Paramount in all situations is the need for the student to feel genuine success. If work is too easy they feel hurt and insulted. 'Is this all you can think I can do?' If work is too hard they experience soul-destroying, confidence-obliterating failure. It is so important for teachers and parents to work with and analyse the student's work, to see where they are at, what they can achieve and what is simply too stressful ... at present. Listen to the child, this is most important thing of all.

Focus on life and social skills

Life skills should be the focus of the curriculum. There are functional skills that students must be able to do before you begin teaching parts of the curriculum that are nice to know as opposed to necessary to know. For example, can they make a phone call? Can they book a cinema ticket online or hand over the correct Euro note when shopping?

Lots of social skills training is required for this particular group of students. Social immaturity and vulnerability, as mentioned above, are obvious. Tailored social skills training with lots of role play can be great fun.

In relation to social skills training, students will need to learn how to transfer this skill into real-life situations. They will have difficulties generalising and using these in different contexts. Never give up. Focus on one skill at a time and chip away at it together.

Academic progress is always successful when there is repetition and practice. The same is true for social skills. Overlearning may seem tiresome but important skills must be embedded though overlearning and revisiting until they are automatic.

Set reasonable expectations

Reasonable expectations need to be set for the child with a moderate learning difficulty. Many parents can be in a state of denial and are simply delusional about their child's academic potential. If someone works themselves into the ground, of course they will achieve 'more than that teacher said they would' – but at what cost and for whom have they done it?

A personal sense of achievement comes from setting a reasonable goal or target that can be achieved with hard work but not exhaustion. Mental health and well-being are our priorities as educators and parents.

Severe to profound learning difficulties

Students with severe to profound difficulties will have impaired awareness of themselves and people around them. Daily tasks may require significant assistance and are often accompanied by other difficulties both physical and neurological.

How to help

Developing skills such as feeding and toileting will be the priority. This student may have many professionals helping them, such as a physiotherapist, occupational therapist, speech and language therapist, and psychologist. This team will work with teaching staff and parents to devise a bespoke curriculum. Their tailored programme should focus on what the student loves and what they can do, and then build from there. As a team, pick a small number of priority skills to focus on, chosen because they are achievable and mastering them will benefit the student. For example, it may be something like feeding themselves with a spoon and learning to use an iPad – things that are going to improve their life.

Once you've picked the priority skills, there are further decisions to make:

- Who will teach these skills?
- Who will reinforce them and where?
- What is the purpose of focusing on these skills?
- How will they improve the student's functionality?
- How will the team measure success?

18

Developmental coordination disorder (DCD)/dyspraxia

DCD is categorised as a physical difficulty but has many emotional and learning implications. It is unfortunately severely underdiagnosed.

Signs to watch out for

- *Erratic organisation*: The student's schoolbag, desk or locker may be comparable to a recycling bin.
- *Dressing*: You've asked them to put their shoes on and as you are about to head out the door, you realise they still haven't located their second shoe! Lack of awareness of a dishevelled appearance is common.
- *Being a messy eater*: A child with chocolate all over their mouth is only cute for the first few years. They may struggle to use a knife and fork and opt for eating with their hands, much to your horror.

- *Poor handwriting is common*: While some students are reported to have lovely handwriting, ask yourself is this coming at the cost of speed? Prizes for handwriting are only given in primary schools. As they progress into the teen years, the pace of classwork increases. Keeping up with taking down notes or copying homework off the board becomes a problem.
- *Clumsiness*: Some students experience clumsiness, e.g. dropping things, bumping into things, falling. They may look awkward when running.

If these things negatively impact on a student's daily life to a significant degree and if these things are not attributable to any neurological difficulties, you can assume they may need to see an occupational therapist. The occupational therapist will put them through some physical tests to see if they have DCD/dyspraxia. Of course as with all difficulties, there is a spectrum. A student may have one very definite trait of DCD, e.g. poor handwriting, but they are excellent at sport. We need to be careful about putting someone into a clearly defined box. I had one student with DCD who played sport at county level. Some people might ask, 'How can someone so good at sport have DCD?' Think of it like a pick 'n' mix sweet shop – it is possible to have a little bit of this and a lot of that.

Dyspraxia is linked to sensory processing difficulties. We all know about our five main senses, but there are two other senses that help us navigate our way through life. These two senses are frequently a little off with students who have DCD.

THE PROPRIOCEPTION SYSTEM

Inside our muscles we have receptors. These are in communication with our brain. They let our brain know where our limbs are. They tell our brain how much effort is required to squeeze that ketchup bottle or how far to lift our foot to reach the step in front of us. This is then recorded into our memory so we can do it again automatically. This is our proprioception system working correctly. Students with DCD have poor proprioception. The communication between their brain and muscles is inaccurate. The student will squeeze the ketchup bottle too hard – the whole thing squirts out and mum yells! They don't lift their foot high enough to reach the step and they fall. They hurt themselves, plus they're mortified, and they cry.

Students with DCD when young can be overly emotional and get upset easily. This is totally understandable. Think of walking across terrain without sure footing. It's scary. If they have hurt themselves a lot, they become fearful. Tears can make the student seem immature for their age. Tears are not cool at school. They may misread how hard they need to kick the ball so they never get picked for teams. All this gives their self-esteem a good thrashing. It becomes a vicious circle and a negative self-fulfilling prophecy. Students begin to opt out of potentially embarrassing situations, choosing to be sedentary and inactive.

The brain will always seek information and feedback from the muscles in the limbs. If the messages are dulled, then there may be extra craving for muscle feedback, and therefore there is a reason why the student is wriggling in class or overly tactile with other students. They can get into trouble for pushing against others, jumping or lashing out, or invading personal space. They are simply fulfilling the need for sensory feedback to their brain.

Of course while this may explain, it doesn't excuse. Students with these traits need to be introduced to alternative strategies, and these strategies need to be practised and repeated before they become automatic (these strategies will be discussed later). Students with DCD may seem heavy-footed, stomping the ground harder than most, or walking on their toes for extra sensation. Again, this is the brain seeking extra clarification about where their limbs are in space.

As mentioned above, if the proprioceptive system is working correctly, the muscles know how much effort or strength is required to dress and move and walk etc. and all these functions get committed to muscle memory and become automatic. If the proprioceptive system is faulty, the student will rely on visual information, looking at the task and making a guess as to how much force or strength is required to put on the sock, lift the bag or walk up the steps. This visual calculation takes time and therefore the student with DCD will be slower at most physical tasks. Little consolation when you're late for work and your child is at the door in full uniform but barefoot!

The vestibular system

This system is connected with the inner ear. Those of you who suffer with vertigo will know how your balance can be affected and how feelings of nausea can occur. The vestibular system is responsible for our balance, direction and movement. Having poor balance is frightening when you have learned that you fall easily. This system is responsible for knowing the degree of movement required to reach an object or move to a certain space. Handwriting is affected by both systems. Handwriting is a succession of movements in this direction and that.

Sensory processing

Students with sensory processing difficulties can be overly sensitive to itchy tags or clothing. Feeling nauseous with certain smells like crisps or perfumes. Their experience of pain may be out of balance. They may feel pain intensely or not enough. Loud bangs may startle them. Bright lights may cause headaches.

How to help

Dressing, tying shoelaces, buttoning a shirt are all directly affected by the proprioception and vestibular systems. It's all about space, distance, application of pressure and pulling. Dressing seems like a childish task, so when it takes a student longer to do it than their peers and they struggle to get these simple life skills fulfilled, their self-esteem is obviously affected. But fear not, I feel that once you can explain the 'why' to the student and they accept themselves for who they are, then they can move onto the occupational strategies to overcome any difficulty. Movement can be fraught with insecurity. Past scary experiences may lead to students with DCD opting out of sporty situations, their self-esteem having had too many beatings in the past. It is always good for students to know the 'why'. Explain the vestibular system to them simply. Explain that they should avoid opting out of sport. Sport is actually the best way to improve vestibular and proprioception difficulties. Poor muscle tone and posture is very much linked to DCD. Students should engage in exercises to strengthen muscles

Practice

One thing I have learned from my daughter is that determination is your biggest ally. Take the skill they cannot master and practise, practise, practise until they have mastered it. Yes, it's taking them longer than their peers but that doesn't mean they won't master it in the end. Alternatively, find an alternative! If handwriting is the problem – type. If it's shoelaces – use slip-ons or Velcro. If it's organisation – use digital reminders. There is always a way. There is nothing to be ashamed of. If they don't like the tags on their clothes – cut them off. If they don't like the ridges on their socks? Wear them inside out. You get the gist.

Desensitising

Sometimes avoidance strategies are appropriate and sometimes they are not. If you are overly sensitive to smells you may make sure you don't sit beside the boy who eats crisps for lunch. What happens when the person with the crisps is someone they like? There is a thing called desensitising. Basically, they have to build up their tolerance levels little by little. If the wool on their school jumper is too itchy, maybe before they start back to school, wear the jumper for 5 minutes one day, 10 minutes the next, 15 minutes the next and so on.

Tell others

They can also explain to people that they have a sensory processing difficulty. They could ask the school if they can wear a different jumper or they could ask their friend not to eat crisps, but it isn't possible to get the whole world to change for them. Yes, they are entitled to certain accommodations in respect of this difficulty, but it's a two-way process. They must also make the effort to desensitise themselves towards certain things they will frequently encounter. My daughter had an aversion to mint toothpaste. She would only use a marshmallow flavour one we found. The dentist confirmed that I wasn't washing her teeth with sugar – it did have appropriate ingredients. We were all happy – that is until the toothpaste was discontinued. She stretched it out as long as she could, sparing the portion, putting a dot on each night, scraping every last bit ... but eventually the tube had to go. So, we worked on having a tiny dot of the standard toothpaste, followed by a slightly larger dot the next night and so on. Don't get me wrong: she hates mint, but she has moved on now to being able to tolerate it.

Patience is key

The key is they have to be patient with themselves and request patience from others. Here is where I'm a total hypocrite! There are many occasions where I have put undue pressures on my daughter to hurry up and be more organised. I have to remind myself that it requires students with DCD extra effort to do the same tasks as their peers, and appreciation should be given to students in relation to this. I guess this makes me a fallible parent. But we can only strive to do better next time.

> **TOP TIPS FOR PEOPLE WITH DYSPRAXIA AT SECONDARY SCHOOL
> (WRITTEN FROM THE EXPERIENCE OF
> A 14-YEAR-OLD STUDENT WITH DCD)**
>
> 1. 'You need your laptop! Your classmates will ask you why you have it. I just said, "Because my handwriting is crap" and they never asked me again.
> 2. Ask to be seated beside a plug in every classroom so you can charge your laptop.
> 3. Ask to get a locker that is at eye level. Have locker dividers. Have a lot of locker keys because they are very easy to lose.
> 4. Have big zip folders, one per subject. Put everything from that subject into that one folder. Make sure they fit all your books.
> 5. Have a large, long, see-through pencil case that makes it easier for you to get your pencils. Only have what you need.
> 6. Put a copy of your timetable on the back of your locker door, in your jacket pocket or your school bag and written in your journal. You could also have a screenshot of it on your phone.
> 7. Ask teachers to email notes or post homework to save you having to write things down.
> 8. Take screenshots of the notes on the board.
> 9. Set a lot of timers, e.g. when to wake up, when to leave the house, when to get to class.
> 10. Lay your uniform out the night before so you can just put it on when you wake up. Have your tie

tied so you can just put it on over your head every morning.
11. Get to know your caretaker – they can be great help with your locker or in general.
12. Make sure your teachers know you have dyspraxia. But sometimes you have to remind them because sometimes they might give out to you for being too slow or for not having the words all down.
13. Homework can take a long time and you may not always get it finished. Have a note from your parents in your journal to explain your situation to your teachers.
14. Ask your parents to get permission from your teachers to let you pack up your stuff earlier at the end of class as it takes you a bit longer.'

19

ADHD (attention deficit hyperactivity disorder)

Far too many books about ADHD focus on a student's difficulties. There is an over-focus on what the child can't do. I want to state, straight off, that most students I know with ADHD could rule the world. Their energy and enthusiasm is inspirational. If they were allowed to focus purely on what interests them, they would be regarded as high achievers. Of course, that is not how the world works and particularly not how the school curriculum works.

So many parents and teachers ask the question, 'Do you think he has ADHD?' Only a trained professional/clinician can make a diagnosis of ADHD. The professional will have a very clear set of criteria (DSM 5 *Diagnostic and Statistical Manual of Mental Disorders*) that a child must display for a period longer than six months before an official diagnosis can be made. Everyone can display traits of ADHD at different periods of their life. Anyone can display ADHD traits in relation to a certain topic that excites them or a group of friends who excites them. We need to be careful not to bounce this term about too much. You are allowed to be a bouncy, lively person.

SIGNS TO WATCH OUT FOR

The traits a professional will look for are:

- Inattention when playing or doing schoolwork or household tasks
- Making silly mistakes
- Not listening to instructions or drifting off when others are talking
- Failing to follow through – always starting things but never completing them
- Losing things
- Failing to tune out other distractions – being easily distracted
- Difficulties with organisation – bag, locker, copies, notes, timekeeping
- Blurting things out
- Fidgeting, squirming, tapping
- Always on the go
- Constantly talking, not giving others a chance to talk and interrupting them
- Making impulsive decisions – acting without thinking

Types of ADHD

The diagnosis will state that ADHD is one of three types:

- *Combined*: traits of both inattention and impulsivity/hyperactivity
- *Predominantly inattentive*: traits of inattention but not impulsivity/hyperactivity
- *Predominantly hyperactive/impulsive*: traits of hyperactivity but not inattention

Like with every topic covered in this book, it is fair to say that ADHD has a spectrum. This ranges from mild ADHD, where a few areas need support, to severe ADHD, where the assistance of a medical team is needed to draw up a programme. Like many learning differences, some days are more 'ADHD' than others, and observations and record-keeping is required to create accurate targets and goals. Your targets cannot be based on hunches or hearsays.

Getting diagnosed

Let's say you have a child who is showing traits of ADHD. You are convinced. What next? If you are a teacher, consult with other teachers and get definite data from observations. You cannot go to a parent and say I think your child has ADHD because they weren't listening to me today. If you are a parent, consult with the school for their opinion. The rule of thumb for any difficulty is to look at what could be worked on yourselves (child, parent, teacher) and draw up an IEP (Individual Education Plan) with targets and methods of reaching the target. If you can see progress, then what need is there to get a diagnosis?

If, however, after many failed interventions, your child is getting into difficulties that prevent them from reaching their full potential or prevent them from sustaining friendships, then and only then is it time to seek the help of a professional diagnosis. Make no mistake, it is up to the school to provide stepped interventions and support, and it is up to the parents to provide boundaries, incentives and reasonable sanctions. Children like structure and predictability. If these difficulties persist to the extent that the rest of the class is prevented from learning or the health and safety of other children is jeopardised, supportive interventions must be put in place. If a member of the family is impulsive/hyper and it is having an adverse effect on everyone, then an intervention or professional advice may be necessary. Maybe a diagnosis will help alter the strategies to ones that are more effective. A professional can give you strategies that have proven to be beneficial to children with ADHD.

How to help

Can ADHD be cured? Again, it is not an illness or defect. It is, like all other topics discussed in this book, a way of thinking and learning.

Highlight the positives

When working on a particular 'thing' as a target for modification, we need to make sure it is enveloped in positives, for example 'I think you are great at bringing joy and laughter to any room you walk into', or 'I love the way you are generous to everyone and would share your last sweet', or 'You've amazing energy', etc. Don't make it up. Children know when you are sincere. Look for the good and highlight it. Only when they feel you are genuinely proud of them, should you introduce the idea of jointly deciding on some possible targets for improvement. Some teachers successfully employ the old method of two stars and a wish (outlining two things that are really good and one thing that could be improved upon). The targets need to be realistic and achievable, otherwise you are setting the student up for failure. If they are disorganised, it is too vague to say, 'Target 1 is to be organised.' It needs to be broken into specific targets for what the end result will look like, and the tasks involved in meeting these targets, for example:

- *Timekeeping*: setting alarms the night before; laying out clothes the night before
- *Equipment*: using checklists, ensuring they have spare supplies
- *Notes*: using folders, having spare copies
- *Deadlines*: using apps or calendars and diaries to visually display due dates
- *Mess*: weekly time dedicated to cleaning out the bag/desk/locker/bedroom

Set clear targets in an understanding environment

All children flourish in an understanding environment. A diagnosis explains but doesn't excuse challenging behaviour. Our approaches to discipline may become a little softer with a lot more structure once we know the student has a learning difference. Set no more than two or three targets: if you want to support ten challenging areas for the student at any one time, what message is that sending to them? Be clear about what you are going to work on. The best place to devise these targets is at an IEP (Individual Education Plan) meeting or maybe having a family meeting without other siblings. They themselves need to believe that this is something that needs to improve. They are unlikely to work on something they themselves don't see as a problem ('It's only Mum/Dad/Teacher who has a problem with it.')

Get them to accept, for example, that being late for school isn't good and is something they need to work on. How can they work on it? Get them to come up with the answers themselves, for example pack their bag the night before, set an alarm and then set another alarm ten minutes before they need to leave the house. Maybe they will decide to target their lack of focus. Get them to come up with strategies to help with this, for example putting a keyring on their desk to remind them to tune in again. Or arrange with their teacher to make a discreet gesture to remind them to get back in the game. Roaring at someone in the classroom to pay attention only serves to humiliate. Students will see efforts to 'change them' as an affront, an unwillingness to accept them for who they are ... and they would be right.

We need to look at why we want a particular behaviour changed. Can we accept this particular behaviour as part of their personality or is it something that needs to be worked on for their own sake or out of respect for others? Will it benefit them by helping them to fit in with friends and family, living with reduced conflict? Will it help them to demonstrate respect for others? Will it help them to give sufficient attention to schoolwork or organisation so that they don't underachieve?

Looking for the positive, looking for chances to reward good behaviour and giving loads of praise is far more powerful an approach than handing down consequences. Positive reinforcements promote good behaviour. The behaviour will then, with enough praise, become automated. Parents and teachers need to be very specific about the praise – just like setting the targets, you should avoid generalisations. For example, if the student concentrated for ten minutes but lost their concentration after that, recognise the success of the ten minutes: 'I noticed that you didn't turn around once in ten minutes and you maintained eye contact with me or the board the whole time I was explaining it – well done you!'

Career guidance

The life of a person with ADHD gets much easier if they choose a career that suits their personality. Would science excite their curious mind? Would acting feed their energetic souls, allowing them to move around and be creative? Would a people-centred career hold their interest, allowing them to meet new person after new person? Would entrepreneurial exploits allow them to thrive, giving them the ability not to overthink things? School, however, is not usually a comfortable place for a student with ADHD. Sit in that desk! Stay still! Focus! The catch-22 is that in order to have their choice of careers, they usually require a good educational qualification – a qualification that matches their intelligence. However, students who do not get appropriate support may underachieve and chose a career based on the best they can get, as opposed to choosing one they will love and thrive in.

Understand the effects of discipline

When students remain undiagnosed, discipline is inappropriate. They become accustomed to being seen as bold and even feed into the self-fulfilling prophecy. 'If everyone says I'm trouble, then I suppose I'll make trouble. That's what's expected of me and it's easier.' There is often a feeling of hopelessness, leading to poor motivation. Being reprimanded and scolded many, many times a day can be detrimental to their self-esteem and self-worth. If they are aware that they seem to drive their peers mad and are often excluded, well that's very difficult to cope with at any age. Hence the need for them to get properly diagnosed and properly supported, with lots of strategies to implement.

Encourage good sleep

Sleep disturbance exacerbates an already difficult situation. We all fly off the handle and are difficult when we are tired. People with ADHD can often find it difficult to get to sleep. They have active minds and so winding down is essential. The importance of good sleep routines cannot be underestimated. Try to avoid video/internet games an hour before bed. Remove devices from the bedroom. Have a notebook in the room so that if they have any burning idea in their head they can jot down a reminder and work on it the next day. This notebook is only for reminders; it should not become a sketchbook for creative ideas. Encourage reading a book at bedtime. Try to get them to go to sleep at the same time each night. Avoid sugary drinks, caffeine and large meals too close to bedtime. Some form of exercise during the day ensures better sleep. Ensure the room is completely dark with blackout blinds. They may resist at first, but doing a meditation or body scan before bed is an excellent way to wind down; there are lots of self-guided meditations and body scans online. Of course remember this will need to be done before they go to bed as you don't want any device in the room.

Clear, consistent, fair boundaries and consequences

Set clear boundaries in times of calm. I say this with full authority as a parent: when I am in the middle of a heated moment, I tend to bellow out the new set of rules that will be imposed from now on! Nothing constructive comes out of shouting and knee-jerk reactions. Make no mistake, every house has pressure-cooker moments that explode, so there's no need to beat yourself up over it. The boundaries need to be set when everyone is thinking clearly and cohesively:

- How much time do we all think should be spent on homework?
- You find it hard to concentrate, so will we work in short but often spurts or do you feel you would work better by getting it all done in one go?
- What do you think the consequences should be if you break a rule that we have set?

Structure and knowing the boundaries is very reassuring to all children. While they may kick back against the 'rules', they do in fact like them. The problem comes when you are not consistent. If they know you don't always follow through, then they will always test the water to see if today is a day you might break. The consistency of boundaries and rules needs to be discussed with all teachers, parents and caregivers. The consistency needs to come from everyone. More than other children, the child with ADHD needs clear, unwavering but fair boundaries.

Along with clear boundaries, the need for clear, non-negotiable consequences also needs to be discussed in times of calm. Allowing the child to have an input into what the consequences of certain actions are means they will gain a sense of control. The consequences should not be too severe, as a student with ADHD will find themselves outside the boundaries more frequently than their peers, so being subjected to too many consequences will have a negative impact on their self-esteem.

Never give up supporting your child towards positive behaviours. Reinforcements and consequences need to be applied consistently, but, more importantly, persistently. Modifications towards more harmonious behaviours will come, just not overnight! Usually, a student will promise you the sun, moon and stars ... and really mean it in that moment. Next thing you know, within an hour, they have broken the agreement you have just made. As frustrating as this is, keep your head, point out the problem, apply the consequences and try again. Forgive and forget! Keep going for the sake of this student and never give up.

Reduce the triggers and discretely keep them on track

Have a good chat with your child or student. Give the student a voice by asking them what would help them to learn. Teachers should ask where in the classroom do they feel they could concentrate more effectively. This leads to the student feeling in control rather than being reefed up to the front of the room like some sort of criminal being punished. Have a chat about friends who seem to bring out the behaviours they are trying to reduce. Teachers don't need to publicly humiliate a student to set an example. If you know your student has ADHD, you know they may frequently lose their place in the book you are working from. It is easy to simply walk by their desk while carrying out the lesson and in a sort of by-the-way manner discreetly point to where they should be in the book as you carry on. The student will see you as kind, fair and supportive. Teaching is not an us-against-them profession. The old days of the scary schoolmaster have thankfully long gone.

Set up a 'glance code'. A simple arranged glance or gesture lets them know you need them back on track with you. Hopefully this habit of keeping on track will eventually become automated and part of their own self-regulation system.

Diet

Take a good look at your child's diet. This can be particularly difficult if the home diet is collectively poor. I'll put this as medically accurately as I can: when you eat crap, you feel crap and you act crap. No matter what way you dress it up, sugary and greasy foods play havoc with the behaviour of a student with ADHD. Start with the supermarket. If it's not in the trolley to start with, you won't have to say no a million times at home. Try to educate them on the benefits of healthy living. Drinking enough water is essential.

Exercise

This is beneficial for lots of reasons. Students with hyper tendencies need to burn off that excess energy. Students with inattention need to shake up their system. When they exercise, they become more alert. It lifts their mood and hence they're more willing to engage in things that are hard. Many students with ADHD have coexisting sensory issues. Exercise provides the sensory feedback students with sensory issues crave. Lots of parents will say, 'My child isn't coordinated and hates sport.' Exercise doesn't just mean competitive or team sports. Running, walking, swimming, exercising to videos, whatever gets them moving will do the trick. If they are coordinated and sporty, count your blessings and cash in on that gift by making sure they are members of clubs and teams, etc.

Movement breaks

This is a tricky one when it comes to the classroom. Many psychological reports state that the student must have movement breaks. So teachers give movement breaks and the student ends up spending half the year walking around the school, at their locker or just heading to the toilet. The amount of movement breaks and their duration need to be recorded to ensure they are not overused. Do the movement breaks need to involve leaving the room or could it just mean putting something in the bin? They are very important but need to be tailored to the student and their frequency monitored. Some students like breaks but for others it can interrupt a flow of learning. They find it hard to get started, so lots of movement breaks mean they have to get started lots of times. Review it with your student to see if it genuinely helps. Ask them what they feel is a fair amount or when they feel they require it most.

The token system

I'm sure some very academically acclaimed people feel that the desire to change behaviour needs to be intrinsic, coming from the person themselves. Of course this is true, but a little abstract for the student to grasp. I'm afraid, controversially or not, I've had great success with a good old-fashioned bribery system ... excuse me ... *token* system. If you do this, you get a token. If you have ten tokens, you get X, Y, Z. It is instant and tangible.

Engage in active listening

As a parent and teacher I am fully aware that when you are listening to children, their arguments can seem ridiculous. I have to remind myself that the important thing here is not to immediately shoot their opinions down. The important thing is that they see you actively listening. A friend of mine, Dr Paula Flynn, has written much about authentic listening. It goes far beyond saying, 'I hear what you are saying but we are going to do it my way anyway.' If you can make a change they suggest, go with it, and in doing so you are displaying the fact that you were authentically listening. In fact, children will never fail to surprise us with their insights into things we had no idea they understood.

Celebrate/acknowledge progress

If a child's target is 'Being more organised', then you will have broken it down into what that would look like. You will have listed the steps needed each night to maintain and achieve the target – put their clothes out the night before, pack their bag the night before, put a note on the fridge about what needs to go into the bag at the last minute, leave their bag and coat at the door, etc. Let's say they have made a great effort five days out of seven. Rather than being annoyed over the two days they were disorganised, acknowledge that unlike a month ago, when everyday was disorganised, they are now organised most of the time. Sure, they will have some days they slip, but let's celebrate their success ... enter praise and tangible reward!

Support groups and education

Try to get your child to be part of a support group for students with ADHD if you feel they would benefit from this. So often I find that parents have practically a PhD on the subject and yet their child knows nothing about ADHD. Running support groups is very useful. These are places where students can share common challenges and experiences, laugh at different anecdotes they share and, more importantly, share strategies that work.

If you do set up a support group within your school or community, they need to be well monitored and the groups may need to be tailored in terms of age and interests. The group dynamics are important. Some older teens have a very advanced life experience that may shock and give a bad example to younger students. However, it is the older teens who benefit the most, as impulsivity can be very dangerous if students are socialising in circles where alcohol and drugs are available. It is better that adults be aware of this, allow students to discuss these situations and allow time for reflection. This is far better than sticking our heads in the sand and conveniently remaining oblivious to any dangerous carry-on.

Students with ADHD may be vulnerable because of impulsivity. Alcohol and drugs intensify the impulsivity. They will need enormous support in making the right decisions and it is good if they have an adult (other than a parent) they can talk to. I will always tell students that what is said in the room stays in the room, unless they are in danger or it transpires someone else is in danger. The adult will obviously have to pass on any information if the child is in any danger in accordance with child protection guidelines and legislation.

20

Organisation and executive functioning

Executive functioning was previously discussed in the chapter on assessment jargon, but if we are discussing organisation and improving these skills, it is important to revisit this topic. The executive functioning system is a set of mental skills required to carry out basic daily life tasks. To have a successful day, I need to roughly plan it in my head. I need to manage my time and stick to a routine. This requires that I employ a set of automated skills to mentally visualise how it's all going to go. It is the sequence of smaller tasks to reach the end task. Getting ready in the morning, for example, requires that I get out of bed, go to the toilet, get washed, find what clothes I am going to wear and put them on the right way around, and it all has to be completed within a certain timeframe. I need to know if I have to hurry up or whether I have loads of time and can take things at a

Organisation and executive functioning

leisurely pace. If I get dressed and head to the kitchen, but then remember that I've to go back to get my jumper and then back to the kitchen again ... well, it's my executive functioning that has let me down. Putting seemingly simple daily tasks in the correct order in an efficient, timely manner is actually quite complicated when you break it down.

The executive functioning system is often known as the control centre of the brain. Remember that the brain is bombarded with lots of sensory inputs. Essential information comes through our senses – sight, sound, touch, taste, smell. We then have to process all of this and establish what is happening. What should I be doing next? Which sensory inputs should I be blocking out and which do I need to pay attention to? What do I need to do next if I want X to happen by 8 a.m.? I have an idea (ideation), but I have to be able to visualise and act out many steps before X actually happens.

When a student has executive functioning difficulties, daily life is actually quite stressful for them. Getting out the door on time is stressful. Making sure they've packed all the correct books, copies and equipment – all stressful when their executive functioning is weak. A student with executive functioning difficulties will often arrive in school without their homework. This is upsetting for them if they spent lots of time on the homework and they know they did it really well. They get in trouble and this can again be very upsetting. Teachers will complain about the lack of organisation. For parents it will seem as if they are constantly having to tell their child to hurry up – 'Did you do this?', 'Did you do that?' The person the student is most upset with is themselves and of course this leads to poor self-esteem and negative self-talk – 'I'm useless. I can't even pack my bag.' Just like everything else we have discussed, it's not OK to just say, 'Oh well, I've poor executive functioning skills, therefore I'm disorganised.'

How to help

Once you've established that the difficulty for your child is actually executive functioning and not a mild dose of 'I couldn't be bothered', then you need to break the challenges down and look at the root of where things are going wrong. Pick one thing to support at a time. You can choose from a number of things, such as leaving the house on time in the morning, getting their homework, books and equipment all into school, or having tidier work. Once you've picked one, then break it down into smaller tasks to be supported. Work on it like building up a muscle that will become automatic.

Make a plan for leaving the house on time in the morning

To make an improvement plan, you need to identify and narrate specifically when it all goes wrong.

Discuss with your child what happens five minutes before they leave the house. Are they running around the house in a panic looking for their other shoe or their schoolbag? Are they getting into the car and then having to go back into the house because they forgot their lunch, or PE gear, as it's Tuesday?

Now, with your child go back and reflect on what happened that morning. Discuss how things could have been improved. Also discuss things they did well and what helped. The children themselves will usually come up with the best answers, such as:

- I'll make sure my uniform, including my shoes, are left out the night before.
- I'll pack my bag the night before and leave it at the front door.
- I'll put a Post-it note on the front door the night before to remind me to get my lunch out of the fridge.
- I'll put a Post-it note on the front door to remind me it's Tuesday and to bring my PE bag.

Let your child know that you are happy to help them with this if they like, but that you're not nagging, just nudging. Ask them if they would prefer to do the improvement plan by themselves or if they would like a little support via reminders and then gradually take it on independently. This gives them back the control.

Make a plan for bringing homework, copies and equipment to class and for meeting deadlines

Sit down together to make an improvement plan. Get a discussion going, where the child can preferably self-identify that there is an issue. Highlight that this is not their fault, but that it needs to be focused on and improved. Again, narrate the scene: what gets forgotten? What are the consequences and what does that look like? Now get them to come up with strategies to prevent this happening. Again, children are usually good at coming up with solutions themselves and may need just a little prompting. Try the following:

- Pre-write 'PE tomorrow' (or any other subject that needs equipment) into their school diary for each week. If PE is on Tuesday, then they should put a reminder in every Monday section of their diary.
- Pre-write assignment-due dates into their diary the minute they get them.
- Do their homework the day they get it and tick it off as it's completed. They should highlight things that remain outstanding, so they can see at a glance what is yet to be completed.
- Leave spare copies/books/equipment at school and at home. This may mean having two sets of maths sets, rulers or pencil cases. It may even mean having two sets of books if they think it would help. Having a digital version at home is always a good back-up plan.

Be honest and realistic with teachers

Teachers will help your child if they know your child is struggling. This is what they are paid to do. It is not a favour. I have found reminding students of this fact very useful. Some students need support in being brave and asking teachers for help. They need to be reminded that teachers are not telepathic. The student needs to inform the teacher if they need something explained again. This is a far better strategy than the student keeping their head down and praying they don't get called on for an answer – that in itself is a stressful situation.

Go digital

Older children could start using the many apps available to input due dates into calendars. Using 'To do list' apps or reminder apps will help them be more organised.

Stick to one spot for homework

If students start their homework at the kitchen table, move to their bedroom later in the evening and then finish off a bit in front of the telly, they now have three places to potentially lose their work. It will also be very unfair to everyone else, as their work is literally spread all around the house. Having one spot for everything is key. When they can't find something, well, there is only one place it can be.

Make a schedule and stick to it

Students need to pick a time to start their homework, a time for a break, a time to restart and a time to finish. You will need to have an honest discussion about what they can realistically fit into their day. It is so healthy for students to be members of clubs and teams, so they need to factor these events into their week. Be careful that students do not have so many activities that getting the required schoolwork completed becomes stressful. Once they have devised a tailored and realistic timetable for homework, you will need to support them in sticking to it. If the approach to homework is unstructured, then panic moments will be common when they realise it's bedtime and they still have three items to complete. Students with poor executive functioning will really struggle to visualise how everything will fit into a timeframe. They will need support in doing this initially. If homework isn't completed simply because they spent the first few hours watching telly, things will need to be revisited. If things are not going to fit because they genuinely don't fit into the amount of available time, then you'll need to contact the school to see if they can make some helpful changes. Homework should be challenging but not stressful. A good teacher will check in to see how long students are spending on their homework. If they are spending too long on your homework it is up to the teacher to differentiate the work. Negotiate this with the student.

Be a little tidier

Some people cope very well in chaos, but for the student with poor executive functioning (poor organisational skills) disorganisation and mess leads to time being spent looking for things under things. I feel children really need a dig-out in this area. I'm not saying go in and tidy their mess up, but keep a 30-minute slot in the week where you go in with them to tidy up their room/study area. Show them how to put things in order. Provide baskets, labels, folders or whatever they need. If you don't provide guidance in this area, you will find smelly socks filed with the English notes under the bed. You'll open the door to a beautifully tidy room only to find that when you open the wardrobe, a whole load of 'stuff' will fall out! Once you help them keep it tidy, they will feel a sense of pride and maybe, just maybe, become a tidier person.

Study area

This needs particular attention. Get them to keep each subject's notes and books in one large plastic folder (different colours for different subjects). Everything belonging to that subject goes into that folder. This includes the random sheets. The folders should either be in their school bag, on a shelf or in a large plastic box – nowhere else. When they finish with one subject, they need to put that away before taking out the next. This will always be a challenge and a bit of an uphill battle, but knowing where to find 'stuff' is essential in being organised and getting on well in school, not to mention the time saved and arguments avoided as you are not having to look for things as you are heading out the door. Lots of people struggle with this – I know I do. My husband often told me the most stressful part of his day was looking for my keys. Well, if that's the most stressful part of his day, hasn't he a blessed life! But having poor executive functioning skills can't just be accepted. The student will always have to come up with strategies to offset the disadvantage. My keys are now always on the key rack we installed ... well, usually!

School bags

What's lurking at the bottom of their school bag? Again, dedicate a once-a-week slot to emptying their school bag. Together, take out the sheets crumpled at the bottom of the bag. I'm sure you'll find the odd sandwich and orange too! Put the random sheets into the relevant folders or else let your child decide that they get thrown away. Throwing things away is a fantastic habit. You simply can't keep everything. If a sheet or workbook is not needed for revision – get rid of it! If you have a budding artist, obviously keep the things they/you love, but again you can't keep everything. Take a picture of it and you'll have it forever – then get rid of it!

Lockers

Now, you can't mortify your child by going in and reefing through their locker in front of their friends. However, you can request that teachers give a gentle reminder to the student to spend a little time sorting out their locker. Encourage them to keep using their plastic subject folders and to keep putting the random sheets into the relevant folders in their locker. It's handy also for them to have a glue stick, as sometimes they can stick the sheets into their A4 notepads or hardback copies. Older students could you use a tablet or phone to take pictures of these sheets and organise them into subject folders. Get them to have the spine of the books facing outwards in their locker so they can see clearly what they are. Keep some spare pens and pencils here too.

Pencil cases

Regularly dump their contents all out and sort it. They should only have what they need. They don't need four yellows and three blues – one of each is all they need. Fuzzy bobble pencils and novelty things ... get rid of them! Overly stuffed pencil cases lead to time lost rooting and rummaging. A clear pencil case is a good idea as they will know exactly where to root.

To finish off this chapter, I am very willing to sound like a broken record: if your child is tired because they are not getting to bed on time or are playing a device before and even after bedtime, they are losing. Who can possibly be organised if they are exhausted. We all forget things and lose things if we are tired. They are winning if their mind is fresh and clear.

21

Anxiety

For our primitive ancestors and just like today, survival was the priority.

FIGURE 1: MASLOW'S HIERARCHY OF NEEDS

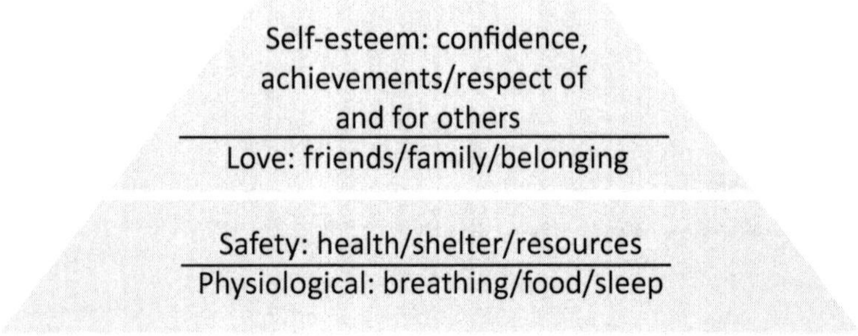

Morality/
creativity/
spirituality

Self-esteem: confidence,
achievements/respect of
and for others

Love: friends/family/belonging

Safety: health/shelter/resources

Physiological: breathing/food/sleep

If you look at Maslow's Hierarchy of Needs theory (see Figure 1), you can see that at the top of the pyramid we are concerned with things like morality, creativity, etc. They are a sort of luxury need and only come into desire after all our other basic needs are fulfilled. A newborn baby's most important concern or need is food. As parents, our most important concern is providing food and housing for our children. Things like building their self-esteem and teaching them skills all come after those basic needs are fulfilled.

Danger alert mechanism

Our ancestors' bodies developed a system for staying alive in the face of threats from wild animals or other hunters. Staying safe requires a danger alert mechanism, and the fundamental element of that mechanism is feeling fear or anxiety. They developed superfast reflexes to detect and deal with these dangers. The body went on high alert. This created physical changes in the body so our ancestors could run faster: senses heightened, adrenaline started pumping and they were in defence mode.

When reading about the brain and anxiety, I decided to do what I always do and break it down into a Ladybird/toddler-friendly version so I could make basic sense of it. So here's my very unmedical version of how and why the brain creates anxiety.

Our brains and anxiety

We have a logical brain (prefrontal cortex) and we have an emotional brain (middle of the brain). When faced with any new situation, we have to figure out: 'Is this a threat or not?' If our amygdala (a little part of the brain) decides there is a threat, then it creates physical conditions in our bodies so we can run faster, etc.

'That's a mouse ... I don't need to run away or kill it. Oh, actually, it's a lion ... run for your life!'

If we need to 'run for our lives', our bodies automatically shut down unimportant functions in that moment (e.g. digestion – hence we get pains in our tummy and our limbs go weak). The unimportant functions shut down so that all our energy can go into running or whatever else is needed to survive. Our hearts start pounding – getting us ready to go. They trigger the adrenaline hormone to be released – ever wonder why people can run so fast when a dog is chasing them? We need this system to protect us in the face of danger.

Fight, flight or freeze

In the face of meeting a wild animal we can fight, flee (→ flight) or freeze (the three Fs):

- Choose to take it on – *fight*
- Choose to run somewhere else – *flight*
- Stay still or hide and it might not see you – *freeze*

Again, these are primal survival reactions.

These dangers no longer exist in our modern lives, but the mechanism of the logical brain and the emotional brain and the control centre of the amygdala still function.

A little bit of worry still has a positive function in our modern lives. If we didn't worry about exams, we wouldn't bother to study and we would fail. It's that little bit of anxiety that makes us study harder. If a parent didn't worry about their children, there would be lots of accidents. Anxious first-time parents experience a primal mechanism to ensure their baby is safe.

Productive anxiety

This feeling of low-key anxiety is functional and productive. It encourages us to do better, as long as it doesn't cross a line and prompt us to drop out. Feeling anxious before going on stage is common for most performers – but they 'feel the fear and do it anyway.'

A little worry keeps us safe, makes us practise harder, etc. If we are worried about a friendship, it can spur us to sort it out, making it a better relationship. If we have a reason, it can be natural to worry, for example if a loved one is sick or we fell out with friends. These situations are natural and mainly temporary.

Problematic anxiety

Imagine, if you like, that there is an emotional brain and a logical brain. The emotional brain sees a massive difficulty where the logical brain sees a minor issue. If a student seems to be worrying for no reason, their amygdala (the little control centre in the brain) may be out of whack! When they experience high anxiety, the emotional brain is winning and they kick into high alert.

If a student worries over little things all the time, this anxiety presents as a challenge. They may need help in the form of simply sitting down with a trusted adult, talking it through and coming up with a plan. Saying something out loud can help the logical brain take back control over the emotional brain. Resilience can take a bit of training. Some children are more resilient than others, but like any muscle, the more you train it, the better it gets. Humans like to be in control, but often we feel we are losing control. That loss of control can lead to incessant concern about what might happen, worrying about something that hasn't even happened ... pre-emptive worry. Everyone has worries and some people are just natural worriers, and that's OK. Anxiety only needs an intervention when it is having negative impacts on the quality of your child's life.

If their feelings are so extreme that it prevents them from having the life they deserve, then you need to intervene. If their period of extreme anxiety lasts longer than six months, they may have an anxiety disorder and need professional help. The first port of call will always be your GP.

SIGNS TO WATCH OUT FOR

Remember, when in high alert, the amygdala shuts down body functions, so if anxiety continues for a prolonged period it can cause tummy aches. Poor digestion means your child could get run down and have a low immune system.

Being in high alert mode all the time is exhausting and hence they may feel exhausted. It interferes with sleep, making their emotional brain even more irrational.

Watch out for the three Fs we mentioned above:

- *Fight*: fighting with loved ones over nothing, losing their temper and overreacting

- *Flight*: running away from any difficult situation, not turning up for a test, refusing to go to youth or sports clubs or even to school
- *Freeze*: going blank when put on the spot about something or asked to read

How to help

Before you decide to get professional help for your child, there are some tangible things you can do to help. The aim is to give your child the feeling that they are back in control, or at least that there is an adult who has their back and will guide them through this difficult time.

Create 'The Plan'

Let's come back to Maslow's theory – food, sleep, connecting with others, etc. Formally sit down in a positive setting with your child. Look at the following elements in their life and come up with 'The Plan'.

Children who are prone to anxiety need to feel in control. They need the adults in their lives to help them with strategies – a plan. This will give the power back to them. If you feel they are not engaging with you, it may be because children often kick back against their parents and we as parents can lose patience quickly. In that case, perhaps it would work better if another significant adult helped them to devise The Plan, for example a guidance counsellor or additional needs teacher in school, or an aunt or uncle or older cousin they connect with.

Jot it down

Once you are both sitting down, ask them to tell you what they are worried about. Tell them that there is nothing too ridiculous. Try and get them to just spit out their anxieties. Sometimes they are worried about the simplest of things that can be sorted out right away. They may have spent weeks obsessing about it. One phone call to a teacher or comment from you that it's not a problem and the weeks of worry end instantly!

The emotional brain is the right side of the brain. The skill of writing uses the left and logical side of the brain. A little problem can be huge in our children's heads until they employ the logical method of writing it down. Once it is written down, they can see – logically – that it isn't really an issue at all and it is nothing to worry about. Explain this process to them. Get them to logically see that it is important to write worries down. Suggest to them to have a little notebook at hand and when a worrying thought comes into their heads, they can jot it down. They can choose to share it with you daily, weekly or not at all. They are in control.

The Plan should address the following areas:

Food

Are they eating the correct foods? As mentioned already, it has long been established that if we eat rubbish, we feel rubbish. Changing long-standing poor eating habits is easier said than done, but it is the most effective way to make them feel better. Nourish your children.

Sleep

A good night's sleep will always benefit the person who has anxiety. It is a vicious circle where the person who worries or is anxious doesn't get a good night's sleep and therefore becomes even more anxious. Please see the section on sleep on pages 9–10.

Is there a TV in their bedroom? Your child is a mini-you. Have you ever binge-watched a boxset? We cannot expect children/teens to have well-developed self-control. They need us as parents to set parameters and boundaries. While they kick back and engage in the power battle, you must show you are in charge in a clear and calm way. Set the rules during the day and not at night time when everyone is tired. Agree together what is fair and stick to it. And while they do put up a fight, children and teens genuinely like to know they live in a safe home with boundaries. A lack of logical rules creates chaos and that's never good for a child or teen with anxiety. They like the security of knowing what's likely to happen.

Toxic relationships

Maybe your child is engaging with toxic friendships. Discuss this with them. Who makes them feel good? Who makes them feel bad? It's naturally better for your child to decide for themselves whom they need to prune and whom they should invest in. However, they may need the obvious pointed out to them. This is tricky territory as banning certain relationships can have the opposite, undesired outcome.

Mindfulness, relaxing, listening to or playing music

If your child suffers from anxiety, they could use one of the many available mindfulness apps and relaxation techniques. These are very useful and many children and teens engage with them and enjoy them.

Some parents have told me that learning to play an instrument was a turning point for their child. Listening to music has long been a method of clearing away the cobwebs of the soul. If you see your child getting anxious, suggest they take some quiet time to listen to some music while lying down or going for a walk. Make it part of the plan. 'When I feel anxious I will do X.'

Exercise

This is a real stress buster. Try to ensure your child has sufficient exercise. It releases anti-stress feel-good hormones, better than any drug. Joining a club has the added benefit of positive social interactions and human connection. However, lots of children and teens find joining clubs and the expectation of performing well at a sport a little too much. This shouldn't prevent them from gaining the benefits of exercise. Walking, running, swimming, bouncing on a trampoline, golf, going to the gym – these are just a few things they could engage in other than team sports.

Explain that everyone is a little crazy!

The mind is wild and complex. Everyone has 'intrusive thoughts'. Crazy ideas or scenarios that get played out in the mind. Your child may feel there is something wrong with them and then fixate on the fact that they've had this worrying thought. It is important that they know that these are only temporary intrusive thoughts.

Finalising and using The Plan

Once you have discussed all the above strategies, you need to talk them through with your child and write it all down in The Plan.

What things in their life are good and what are they going to invest a little more in? This could be friendships, spending time with family, clubs, etc.

What are they changing? Diet, exercise, toxic friendships, digital schedules, etc.

If they are feeling anxious, what are their go-to strategies? Communication with a trusted adult, jotting worries down, exercise, mindfulness, music, change of diet, etc.

Write it all down in a grid. Get your child to type it out, but only list the things they genuinely feel they would use or do. It can't be a work of fiction or something they are creating to please you. So often as I'm writing plans with teens, I will stop and say, 'Do you really think you would do that ... genuinely?' If the answer is yes, then great. If it is no, well, it's better to be honest.

This plan is a comfort in itself. Dig it out every now and then. Revise it according to their feedback. The process itself is more powerful than the piece of paper. It gives them the feeling that at least something is being done: 'I'm not just stuck here.'

A word of warning

These help strategies are your starting point – the support you can give. However, if their anxiety leads to self-harm, serious ideations or other worrying behaviours, you need to seek professional help. Make an appointment with your GP who will then direct you to the best services in your area.

Just show up!

Attendance at school is an enormous hurdle for some students. Unfortunately, it's one of those vicious cycle things. They feel anxious about school because they feel they are behind others, so they avoid school, so they fall further behind ... so they feel more anxious ... and so on.

It's very common for students with learning difficulties to fake illnesses as a means of avoiding the dread of school life. In fact, sometimes they are not faking it at all, as the worry and anxiety can lead to serious digestive difficulties and headaches. Sleep deprivation can mean that they may simply not be fit for school. Some students don't even bother to fake it. They just plain old refuse to go to school.

Here's the thing: your child must go to school if at all possible. Here's where you must hold strong and be tough. Any sign of weakness and you'll experience months of repeated fake illness performances. They must know that you are never OK with them opting out.

Sometimes learning difficulties are impossible to diagnose, as you don't know if the gaps are due to a learning difficulty or created by what they have missed due to absenteeism.

It's always good to have a chat with them and explain the whole fight or flight model. School avoidance is flight and leads to the student falling further behind.

They must understand that it is only a short-term fix and counterproductive in the long run. This must be discussed and accepted. However, you can't just be cold and say, 'Toughen up ... in ya go!' It is essential that you give your child some control. From your perspective the conversation should go something like this:

Yes, you are going in today. If you are still ill by lunchtime, get the school to ring me and we can see where we go from there, but what we need to decide is how we can make life better for you. I can write a note or ring your teacher. Just let me know what you think might help.

- *Do you want teachers not to ask questions of you in class for a little while?*
- *Do you want me to make sure the teacher doesn't ask you to read in class?*
- *Do you want them to give you shorter homework?*
- *Do you need somewhere to go at lunch time?*
- *Is there an issue with a friend that we could help you sort out?*
- *Can YOU come up with any ideas about what could help?*

My children always say that they would need to be bleeding or hospitalised before I'd give them a day off. Of course, when the school rings to tell me they are sick and need to go home, the guilt kicks in! My point is that showing up is so important. School friends are fickle – if your child isn't in, their friends move on, leading to isolation. Some subjects like maths are cumulative so if your child misses one of the foundation blocks, they are just not able to build on it.

To summarise, be strong, send them to school. Work relentlessly with their school to ensure the environment is adapted appropriately, so your child experiences some success and is happy. Remember, teachers are obliged to ensure a child with a learning difference is catered for so keep communicating to ensure success. School avoidance only leads to further isolation, feeling disconnected and widening the learning gaps.

Some anxiety conditions, mental health issues and indeed physical health issues are so great that attendance is not advisable. This call will be made between the parents, the GP and the student themselves. If going to school will cause more damage than not going to school, child welfare must always be paramount. I would say, however, that if you are allowing them to stay at home because you feel they simply are not fit for school, then I would suggest not allowing them to have devices such as phones and games during the school hours. Some students realise that staying at home without a device is no fun and decide to brave going into school instead.

22

Autism spectrum

Two quotes from my students have really stuck with me:

> My biggest disability is other people not understanding.

> My friend told me I didn't look like someone who has autism.

We can fight and protest and say 'this is a disgrace' and 'that is a disgrace', but the reality is that we need to accept that there isn't sufficient information out there about all the various learning differences and, therefore, we can hardly be annoyed at people for their lack of understanding.

Autism is a way of thinking, a way the brain works. Not worse, not less, just different, and let's not overdramatise this: not that different!

There are a range of traits associated with ASD. ASD stands for 'autistic spectrum disorder'. However, I'm definitely not a fan of the word 'disorder'. People with AS need to identify with it, be proud of who they are – who can be proud of having a 'disorder'? But that's a rant for another day!

TERMINOLOGY

Asperger's is a term also used. I think it would be helpful to share a little background information about the evolution of autism/Asperger's terminology. Clinicians use the *Diagnostic and Statistical Manual of Mental Disorders (DSM), a book published by* the American Psychiatric Association, to make a diagnosis. Up to 2013, its fourth edition (*DSM-IV*) was used and it identified Asperger's as a separate diagnosis to autism. Asperger's was regarded by many as high-functioning autism. Clinicians distinguished between Asperger's and autism based on the child's language. According to *DSM-IV*, children with Asperger's do not always have the same speech delay as children with autism.

The latest and revised *DSM* (*DSM-5*) was published in 2013. It does not distinguish between Asperger's and autism, and instead brings them together under the umbrella of 'autistic spectrum disorder'.

NO TWO PEOPLE ARE THE SAME

It seems so obvious, but still needs to be said. Just like any other learning difference, no two people with autism are the same. Students have commented to me how hurt they have felt when they were excluded from a group. When other students were asked, 'Why the exclusion?', they said they didn't think people with autism liked crowds. While some people don't, I have lots of students who are social butterflies. Yes, there can be the odd comment they make that is a little out of context or they miss some of the meaning of the conversations as it was wrapped in linguistic subtleties. But this doesn't mean they don't want to join in. There are lots of autistic traits and each person (and not just students with AS) is somewhere on the spectrum line for each of these. It's like those DJ mixer machines: the unique combination of all those knobs (traits) creates the personality.

Signs to watch out for

The following is a list of common challenges a person with autism may have. Keep in mind all the time that each child will have a very unique set of characteristics. Some areas discussed below may present as intense difficulties, while some do not present as difficulties at all.

Communication/social interaction/reading body language

Your child or student may struggle to speak and take a long time to process language. Some children may be poor at reading body language or facial expressions. This leads to people thinking they are not listening to what others are saying. Reading body language is an integral part of communication. Take a scenario where the child has been talking a lot and it's time to let someone else get in on the conversation. The subtleties of knowing that Mum/Dad/teacher/friend is a little irritated about them talking too much will be visible through facial expressions. However, if reading facial expressions is an area they find difficult, they may find themselves unintentionally annoying friends and family.

Sensory processing difficulties

They may have heightened senses and struggle with itchy tags on clothing, increased feelings of pain or not feeling enough pain when hurt. They may be overly sensitive to smells, tastes and sound. Co-morbidity is when two conditions co-occur together. Lots of children with autism get a diagnosis of SPD (sensory processing disorder), or DCD (developmental coordination disorder/dyspraxia) first.

Information comes to us through our five senses. If these senses are overly efficient, their brains can be overloaded. Smells may be overwhelming, making them feel nauseous. A small bang of the door may sound like an explosion and be very upsetting. A simple bump may really hurt. They may squeeze someone too hard when giving a hug, as their perception of a gentle hug isn't the same as that of the person receiving the hug. Most autistic children I know love a cuddle from their loved ones and we need to be careful not to stereotype people. However, you can understand that if you are very sensitive to touch, the huggy people of this world are a little scary! If you are in a corridor at school, the hustle and bustle of the sound of people chatting and laughing can be exciting and fun. For some students who are sensitive to sound and touch, the noise is overwhelming, and with everyone squashed in a corridor they may be on high alert for an accidental bump. One way of coping with this may be to zone out. This may come across as aloof, but it is a simple self-protection mechanism.

If a student appears to lack empathy when another student is in distress or is upset, or if they aren't great at doing the thoughtful things, remember this student may be dealing with a sensory overload at that time, so forgive them if they miss out on the subtle signs that alert us to other's needs – they are simply preoccupied with dealing with their own challenge.

Motor skills

We have gross motor skills (the ability to run, jump, cycle, open doors, get in and out of cars) and fine motor skills (pinching with our fingers to pick up a pen or use a knife or fork, button a shirt and tie a shoelace). Every physical thing we do requires a gross or fine motor skill. These motor skills are discussed in more detail in the chapter on DCD/dyspraxia. Students with gross motor difficulties may avoid sports that involve kicking and jumping. They could miss out on being part of sports teams as they may always get picked last or not picked at all. Why show up to a club where they know they are going to have their self-esteem kicked? Fine motor issue present themselves in the form of handwriting that is very difficult to read or they may have difficulties with basic personal care tasks.

Personal hygiene

The child or student may refuse to shower or follow basic hygiene routines. Some personal hygiene difficulties may be attributed to poor motor skills, as discussed above. If they have difficulty reaching the back of their head to wash their hair properly, then personal hygiene will become an issue. One student explained to me that the shower spray felt like needles on their skin and they didn't like the feel of it. For others, poor hygiene is linked to poor self-esteem and a poor sense of self-worth. They simply don't see the point of making the best of themselves. In terms of social connections, personal hygiene is a priority. Nobody wants to be friends with the smelly child, so of all the battles that you need to win, this is the one. Again, I must point out that most people with autism or sensory issues have no personal hygiene difficulties. I am including it here, however, as it is a common challenge for many children and parents. Children with sensory imbalances are not choosing to smell: the toothbrush may just hurt their gums, they may dislike the feeling of coldness when they strip, and so on. Remember that quite often children have poor self-esteem. Having pride in our personal appearance is embedded in this aspect of our personality. If we feel worthless, well, we might not feel the need to bother putting time into self-care. Whatever the cause of the poor hygiene, this is one challenge that must be overcome. Small children will call others out on personal hygiene – 'You smell!' – while teens will simply exclude. Other students have the right to complain if the body odour of the person sitting beside them is overwhelming.

Stimming/self-soothing/self-regulation

Stimming is short for self-stimulation. Stimming takes the form of rocking, flicking fingers, tics such as making a noise or repeating a word, etc. These are behaviours we are all familiar with. How many people do you know who twirl their hair or rub their knees or rock ever so slightly? Some people tap their feet or fingers, some bite their nails. These are all self-soothing behaviours and not exclusive to people with autism. When stimming is more intense, the behaviour may stand out as different to their peers.

People who stim should never be asked to stop stimming. One form of stimming will simply be replaced with another. These behaviours are in fact a way of turning down the volume or some sensory overload – like when the student is doing group work and things get loud. The stimming behaviours can intensify in times of stress, for example, if there is a test coming up. There is nothing wrong with employing a strategy to help you to cope with a situation.

Flexibility

The child may find a change in routine very upsetting. In a world where your child is challenged by an onslaught of sensory input, the only way to deal with it is to get ready mentally, but when changes happen, the student will suddenly feel ill-prepared and therefore out of control and vulnerable.

The child may seem unable to let small things go. One very loving mother described her daughter as being as flexible as a steel pole! This is a challenge for both parties. Some may have a tendency to point out mistakes that other children are making. While they may be factually correct, it definitely doesn't do anything for their popularity ratings.

Intense behaviours/special interests

We all have special interests, so at what point is it a problem? The rule of thumb is *nothing is a problem unless it negatively interferes with daily living*. If the special interest is all they can think about and is bordering on obsession, it is therefore a problem. If it's just an interest that they are a little intense about and talk a little too much about, well, is that really a problem once family and friends are OK with it? If your child is talking constantly about this topic to the extent that they are unable to sustain friendships, then some social skills training needs to be introduced.

How to help

Communication/social interactions

Wait time

In the chapter on dyslexia, we discussed that language happens in the left side of the brain. If a child is right-side dominant, then it may take them longer to process language, comprehend it and find the correct words to respond or reply to a question. The next thing they know people have moved on from what they were saying, and the child learns to opt out. Why bother if it is all going faster than their language-processing system can cope with? It is so important to give 'wait time'. Allow your child to process what has been said and give them wait time to allow for their response before jumping in to 'help' them find the words they need. Because of this extra effort required, it may be difficult for them to express what they want to say. Clinicians will always ask if there was a delay in speech when the child was little. When they were little, the frustration of not being able to use words to express their needs may have led to what is horribly, but commonly, referred to as a meltdown.

Cue cards

If words are coming at them left, right and centre and their brain is overloaded, children will simply give up or opt out. Sometimes when we are explaining things to students, we talk and talk and talk. To some students this is simply white noise ... blah, blah, blah. When this is the case, it is very useful to have laminated cue cards on a keyring. These cue cards will have a visual that corresponds to a communication such as:

- Take out your books
- Start writing
- Start eating
- Have quiet time

You should also have cue cards for them to communicate with others:

- I need help
- I need a break

Whatever the common instruction you give your child/student, put a graphic on a little card and, instead of overloading them with words, you can simply point to the graphic. This is very useful for checking their morning routines. If you point to the visual checklist, they can simply say yes or no as you point to the visuals – food, drink, hair, teeth, clothes, shoes, lunch, bag, etc.

Be direct and clear with your child

I have found that your directions and instructions need to be concise and clear with children who have autism.

Body language cues

Educate your child about body language

Like any muscle you work on, it can get stronger. It doesn't have to be some expensive programme. Simply pause the telly on a particular scene and ask your child to read the body language of the two characters: 'Do you think he is angry? How can we tell? What should the other person do next?'

Educate your friends and family

Friends and family need to know that reading body language may be a struggle for a child on the autistic spectrum. They need to be informed that this may come across as selfish, rude or even hurtful. The key is to accept and reframe it as a 'difficulty with body language' as opposed to 'rude'. I often find it is good for children to practise telling people that this is an area of weakness, as it may help them when they get into the wider world of work and relationships. It is also important for family to kindly point out if they have been offended, otherwise how can the person avoid this happening again? Obviously this is tricky and the person with autism can feel offended. Pulling them up all the time is counter-productive and leads to poor self-esteem. People with autism can be brilliantly kind and notice things that no one else will. Others struggle with empathy and may come across as selfish. It is important to know this is not selfishness.

Most people with autism I know are very social. They enjoy interactions and chats. Challenges may arise if they make an ill-timed or out-of-context statement due to the difficulties mentioned above. This again is why it is so important to work on improving the society our children live in, as opposed to 'fixing' the child with autism. Friends and family need to shrug off some ill-timed statements, acknowledge them and move on. Similarly, I have had students tell me that no one calls for them or invites them anywhere. When their peers were questioned about this, they told me that they had done so two months ago, but the invitee hadn't seemed interested. The key thing for their peers to know is that if their classmate says no once to a social interaction, it doesn't mean you don't ask again. Good people with a good understanding of autism will ask every now and then and not give up. This is not to be mistaken for nagging or harassment. Students with autism have the right to decline friendships they don't feel comfortable with, just like anyone else. It is important to ensure your child/student has genuine friends who accept them for themselves. I feel it is important that teachers, peers and friends are informed and educated about appropriate reactions to certain situations. The development of a genuine understanding of others is equally the best gift we can give someone with autism. Of course, some parents/children decide that they do not want their peers or educators informed or instructed, and that's their right also.

Sensory overload/sensitivity

Adjusting the environment

It is very easy to cut the tags of clothing or turn socks inside out to alleviate any sensitivity issues for the child. There are now lots of establishments acknowledging the sensitivities of people who have autism by providing autism-friendly hours at movies and theme parks for example. Schools are now examining their environments to ensure they are autism-friendly by providing safe spaces of quiet and calm.

Educating others

Making sure teachers, family and peers are aware of sensory challenges will make life a little easier. Once children understand that another classmate is struggling with the noise level for example, they will be more accommodating. They may be more aware and therefore support their classmate if they spot them becoming overwhelmed with a sensory challenge.

Desensitising

This is exposing a child to something they dislike on a very gradual basis. If they don't like baths or water, maybe work with them to dip a toe in today, an ankle in next week and the knee the following week. Desensitising a child to some aversions may make life a little easier. Allow the students to see the logic behind a desensitising task. I asked one student if there was anything he would like to become desensitised to. He replied, 'The smell of crisps as it stops me sitting beside friends.' So he worked on smelling a bag of crisps for a few seconds every day and gradually increased the time. I doubt he will ever like the smell, but it is now tolerable.

Motor skills

Find the right club

The trick is to find some club they can engage in that isn't dependent on motor skills. So many children can thrive in technology clubs, chess clubs, debating or student councils. Remember that many children have poor self-esteem and presenting themselves to these clubs is daunting. It may be up to the adults in their lives to seek out initial opportunities.

Use technology

Fine motor skills impact largely on handwriting and basic care skills like dressing. Depending on where they are on this spectrum, there is nothing that cannot be improved upon. If the handwriting is really poor, then there are fabulous voice-to-text apps and software packages out there that will simply sidestep that problem. It is important to seek the advice of your additional needs teacher or clinician to see what programmes they recommend and use in the school.

Practise and use alternatives

If dressing is difficult, they can persist and get better at it – every skill improves with practice. If it is causing stress or taking too long, simple discreet alterations can be made. Seek out Velcro or slip-on options for shoes. Alter shirt buttons that can't be seen under a jumper with those little press clips. Sit down with your child, show them options (not with words, but with physical options – show them the clips or the shoes) and let them choose. Remember to reintroduce difficult tasks as they get older. They can't really wear Velcro on everything forever. As the child grows older their physical strength and dexterity can increase, so never abandon tasks completely. We can create alterations to make life easier in that moment in time but ultimately, it is best to revisit tasks again with a more mature child.

Personal hygiene

Be explicit in a time of calm

There is no point getting into an all-out battle as you drag your child off to the shower. Many screaming matches have been had over showers and nothing is ever solved in this way. A social story needs to be created at a time when they do not need one. Point out the logic of having a shower. What happens when they don't have a shower? Show pictures of people who are neat and clean and others who are not. Would they think it was fair if someone who really stank sat beside them?

Make a plan and stick to it

No bargaining. If they are small, decide on the minimum amount of times they need to take a shower or bath, maybe two or three times a week. Set a time and religiously stick to it.

If you are dealing with a teen, they need to be washing every day. Even if the bath or shower is every second day, the main private bits need to be washed every day. How often does their hair need washing? Are they managing to rinse the suds out properly? Maybe if you put a mirror in the shower so they could see the suds, would that help? Do they need a checklist for the shower, such as rinse, suds, rinse and rinse again?

How often and how well are they brushing their teeth? This needs to be supervised at first. So many children brush the front four teeth and the gums at the back are left to grow spuds. Figure out what the problem is. Is the toothbrush too big or too hard? Is the toothpaste too strong? Give them back the control to choose what would help. Make a shopping trip out of it.

Stimming

Examine their environment

Sometimes children may put their hands over their ears to reduce the sensory overload. The question, therefore, is not, 'How do we stop this child stimming?', but rather, 'What can we manage in relation to their environment that will reduce their sensory overload?' Could they leave class five minutes early to avoid the hustle and bustle of the corridor? Should we go shopping at a quieter time? Take a look at the environment rather than the child. Ask yourself, is there anything wrong with the stimming?

Accommodate them appropriately

Sometimes stimming is a result of being excited or overjoyed – their emotions are running high. What's wrong with stimming in this scenario? Do we want them to change simply because it looks odd to others? Some children pace up and down a room. Is this a problem for others ... well, yes, if it's in front of the TV, but can't we organise a different area for pacing? Children will often talk to themselves, replay events during the day, practise imaginary scenarios. These are important dress rehearsals and should not be met with negative responses. They don't hurt anyone. However, you and your child need to decide if it would be better to have a specific place for talking to themselves, as it may be distracting to others. We also have to allow for the fact that they may really want to fit in. Saying the world should accept them for who they are is simply idealistic.

Explain to others

The people who surround your child need to be educated about stimming. Obviously, the child's behaviours can't have a negative impact on others, for example, if humming is your child's chosen method of self-stimulation, then this can negatively affect the ability of the child sitting beside them to concentrate. Here a viable alternative will have to be discussed and worked on. In my experience, students who stim have no problem explaining how they stim, the situations they do it in and how it helps. They will enjoy coming up with an alternative if it is discussed in a conversation that is accepting and understanding as opposed to pointing out a negative practice.

Avoid them hurting themselves and others

Being totally OK with stimming may not always be the right solution either, particularly if the student's language skills are poor. Perhaps it is a sign that this student is dealing with something medical, like a migraine. Perhaps they are not coping with stress. Is the chosen form of stimming hurting them, for example banging their head or overly biting their nails, or pulling hair? So while we should never stop stimming, we should always ask ourselves, why are they stimming? Are they in any distress or pain and is it having a negative impact on anyone else?

Flexibility

Give them structure and routine

There is great comfort in knowing that 'this thing' is going to happen at this time and 'that thing' will happen at that time. Lots of children with AS find the 'first X, then Y' approach very useful. It gives them forewarning about what is going to happen. There is comfort in structure and routine. There is comfort in knowing what comes next. Their environment, of course, should be adapted as much as possible to facilitate this for your child. Visual timetables and schedules are very useful. Preparations and forewarnings need to be given if there are going to be changes in a day, a substitute teacher, or a day when Mum or Dad are away. They may need it to be marked on the calendar or be given the name of the alternative teacher or minder. This offers control and security. Of course, life is anything but predictable and forewarnings are simply not always possible. This is very uncomfortable for children with autism who require high levels of routine. There may be an emotional outburst that expresses their discomfort with a change of routine or schedule. Creating social stories (a method devised by author Carol Gray) is an excellent way of preparing students for events they may find unsettling, such as starting a new school or going to a hairdresser. The story produces the event, explains it, gives visuals and suggests appropriate ways of dealing with it. Therefore, when the event takes place, it isn't new and scary.

Expose them to some unscheduled events

While we can provide as much forewarning in school and at home as possible, the society in which they will be working and living is far less obliging, and children will need exposure to unscheduled events to get them used to this and to learn how to cope. Maybe they have to learn the language to explain to peers and co-workers in years to come about the need to let them know if there are any changes coming up. Many of my students have found Transition Year (a year where there are many groups and outings and events) very uncomfortable; it is, however, great social skills training for the real world. For example, they had to cope with their scheduled maths class being cancelled because the school had a speaker coming in.

Teach them that other people have different opinions to theirs

A child may want something one way because that is the way they feel it should be, for example where the cereal box goes or what programme gets watched at a certain time. Their refusal to have it any other way may come across as selfish and inflexible, but the child with autism is not out to offend anyone or get the upper hand. There may, and I really do mean *may*, be an inflexibility trait that comes across as stubborn. We need to understand this, but we can only go so far in terms of understanding. Social skills training with the use of social stories, role play and examples are needed to show that other peoples' opinions will differ from theirs. They will have to learn to deal with difficult situations, some of the time. Most of the time, however, if it's no big deal, then why not let the cereal box go there? We all have our own little quirks that other people let go and may even find endearing!

Intense behaviours/special interests

Teach them social skills

Social skills need to be explicitly taught. Awareness needs to be developed around the fact that they need to vary topics. If their special interest is all-consuming, you may need to work with the student on some time boundaries for engaging in and talking about it. Of course it is a joy for that special interest to one day become a career e.g. technology, history or science. Teach them that they need to ask others questions about their pastimes and show interest in them. This may require role play and practice. You may need to provide them with general questions they could use to show interest in others.

Outline explicit timeframes for them. For example, if there are three people in their group, they get only one-third of the talk time.

I have observed students with autism making some lovely friends but because of their poor ability to pick up on body language and social cues, they may overstay a visit or call or text too many times. A friend who has a proper understanding of autism will be able to be gentle and direct with their friend; to explain what they regard as an appropriate amount of texts or visits, etc. and stick to that. Social skills training is at its best when it comes kindly from genuine friends who have an accurate understanding of autism. It is down to us adults to ensure their peers have the opportunity to develop this understanding.

Before we decide to start 'fixing' the traits, proper observations and records need to be taken. It can be one teacher's opinion that the student is standing way too close to people, but it may not be another's. It may have only happened once and that teacher may have then decided to make it their mission to address this. Teachers or parents should observe the behaviour of concern, study it for frequency and intensity and then decide if it is actually a problem or something that we should accept as the student's character. We can't just dive in and start changing things we want to change in a person. Only once it has been quantified as being a problem with proven records should it be tackled with tailored social skills training.

Sometimes children may get too close or stand too far away from others. This is linked to the sensory issues discussed earlier. If a student is sensory seeking (their sensory system is under-stimulated), they may stand too close to others and peers may find this very intense. This challenge of personal space needs to be observed and recorded. If it is in fact a genuine difficulty, then social skills training will need to be carried out explicitly. A small hula hoop around them is an effective strategy to start off with. Use a real hula hoop to give them a concrete picture of what is an appropriate amount of personal space. Get them then to visualise or imagine this hula hoop around them when they are with their peers. Of course you will need to explain that there will be lots of times when breaking this personal space circle is appropriate.

I will always come back to the necessity of educating the community of people that surround your child. The students with autism that I have worked with are acutely aware that they have been excluded at some stage, or indeed maybe during all stages of their lives.

'Every time I joined the group they just stopped.' I have found younger ages less accepting, as older students begin to have an awareness of the right to be different and are open to being educated on the topic. It is essential that the environment changes to suit the child as opposed to the child changing to suit the environment. As always, there must be balance. If a student is offending others or causing some discomfort to them, they must learn by the most effective and explicit means possible that their behaviour must change.

Living in the community

The purpose of all the therapy, programmes and support offered to children with autism is to equip them with the skills to make their living in society easy and enjoyable.

They are *not* a means to change and therefore cure their 'symptoms'. With this said, it seems so blatantly obvious that if we are to accept the person with autism for who they are, then it is not just they who need to practise and modify life skills in order to struggle less. It is essential that their peers and the communities they are a part of first understand and then modify *their* skills to facilitate that member of their community. We spend so much time on the student, getting them to adapt to their environment, and unfortunately forget the other side of the coin, which is equally as important – the community. What work do we do with society to ensure and develop this vital understanding and acceptance? I could rant on, saying that the current situation and people's attitudes are a disgrace. Change starts with one person. Could you engage in some sort of programme around awareness in your community? There are lots of organisations out there that can give support, talks or advice. In our school we have an Ability Week. Could you make sure that all students in your school have an accurate lesson on what autism is?

23

Speech, language and communication

I need to stress here that I am not a speech and language therapist and can only share with you my interpretations and experiences of these difficulties.

Speech refers to the mechanics of making sounds to produce language. We use language to communicate. We have to learn how to literally get our mouths and tongues around the production of sounds that match a meaning – words. It means learning how we use tone of voice and intonation to communicate an intention, learning how we can slow things down or speed them up to give different meanings.

Inability to express how children really feel or what they really want to say leads to frustration and self-esteem issues.

There are two parts to *language*:

- Expressive language – what you say
- Receptive language – what you understand from what others say

The aim of the game is communication. The ultimate purpose of it all is the communication of ideas, feelings, information, instructions and opinions.

Expressive language

We use speech to express ourselves. We use words, sentences, body language and tone. This is expressive language, used to convey intentions and opinions, give instructions, share feelings and supply information. We can hear if someone has a stammer, a lisp or is struggling to get words out.

Receptive language

Receptive language is receiving and understanding the messages we get from other people talking. It means understanding their words, sentences and tone. Language difficulties are often hidden difficulties: unlike speech difficulties that can be heard, receptive language difficulties can't be seen or heard. One early sign of good receptive language skills is when a baby swings around when they hear their name. We learn to understand words and sentences. We begin to understand stories and are able to process it all fast enough to keep up and grasp what is going on as we hear it. We develop the ability to understand instructions or a sequence of tasks to be followed. This receptive language evolves with the child. The child will listen to and understand simple fairy tales. As the child grows, they should begin to be able to comprehend more abstract stories. They should understand underlying meanings in stories. A small child can follow one or two instructions at a time; an older child should be able to remember more instructions. This is linked to working memory – the ability to remember things mentally.

Speech and language difficulties: signs to watch out for

Difficulties in speech may present as a stammer, a lisp and pronunciation and articulation difficulties. Some other, more subtle signs are:

- *Tone*: Does the child have the emotional intelligence to use tone correctly? Their politeness, gentleness, confidence and competence can all be detected in the tone of speech. Can they manipulate their tone in different social situations, being formal or relaxed, witty or serious depending on the situations?
- *Non-verbal signals*: The ability to match non-verbal signals with speech is an essential skill. Do they make eye contact and appropriate facial expressions? Are they able to cope with taking turns when speaking, getting in there when there is a gap and having the courtesy to allow others to have an equal share of the talk time?

Language is both using words to express ourselves and receiving and understanding words to interpret meanings and intentions from others. Language difficulties are severely under-recognised. When a child can't spell, the evidence is before you, on the page. When a child struggles with reading, you can hear it. Children with language difficulties learn to nod in all the right places or develop other decoys, such as misbehaving to distract you from calling them out.

Difficulties with language may present in the child as:

- Prolonged use of childish language in relation to the child's age
- Lack of detail when telling or writing stories
- Delay in sentence formulation, leading to long pauses
- Misunderstanding instructions

Some difficulties are hidden. Students may appear frustrated or disengaged. They may use lots of words like 'em', 'ah' or 'yoke'. They may have long pauses and then literally forget what they were being asked. They may get lost in what they themselves were talking about: 'Wait ... what was I saying?' They may have blank expressions on their faces because they are still processing what you said two sentences ago. They may continue to use childish or basic language even as they get older: 'It was nice', 'I like X'. Students may repeat words in essays because they don't have a large bank of alternative words. They may simply not understand the words in the questions. This results in them coming to school with incomplete homework, which sets them on a discipline route.

To save face, they may start to act out in an effort to distract from what they see as their stupidity. Children sometimes choose the opposite reaction to acting out. They may withdraw, staying completely quiet in class, head down, with the hope that no one will notice them. They may mitch or refuse to go to school. They may become self-conscious with their peers, laughing along with jokes they don't get, and may eventually choose to withdraw from the group. They may choose to be the 'clown', entertaining others with their own one-person show that doesn't require two-way communication.

Speech, language and communication is hard! There are endless ways of putting sentences together correctly. We just pick them up as children – we don't know how or why we say sentences in certain ways. It's only when we meet a non-native English speaker that we realise they are putting sentences together incorrectly. But what if we have difficulties just picking up these grammar rules and semantics correctly as children? What if we don't naturally grasp the social rules of knowing how to take turns or to speak at appropriate volumes? What if we don't automatically learn how to use intonation, or how to use stress and emphasis to make language work for us and to be a good communicator?

Vocabulary deficits

We have, on occasion, had students with perceived language difficulties, but on further investigation it was found that these students in fact had vocabulary deficits. This can be down to difficult life circumstances where children were deprived of verbal input as babies and toddlers. Children need to be spoken with and read to. When toddlers go through their phase of endless questions of 'What does this mean?' or 'What does that mean?', they need to know that the adult in their life will give them an answer. This teaches them to ask again. A wonderfully rich bank of vocabulary is built up. Receptive language thrives in houses where there are lots of conversations, where extended vocabulary is used in everyday interactions. No parent intentionally deprives their child of building up their vocabulary. We all come from different backgrounds. Some adults simply do not have rich vocabulary themselves. This is where books can be used. *Children need to be read to*. Some students with hearing difficulties or persistent ear infections as children may also miss out on this formative period of vocabulary building. The fact is, however, that language is a life-long process. We are always learning new words or trying out new intricacies of speech.

How to help

Like all other topics we have discussed, the plan to help a child needs to be tailored. As with all other learning differences, observation and recording are our first steps. Do we just have a hunch that there is a speech and language difficulty, or do we know? Once we have established that there is a difficulty, it is good to go about seeking professional support. Your GP or health clinic are helpful in supporting you with starting the process. However, the waiting lists are long and there are things that you can do in the meantime to support speech and language. From your observations you will be able to make a priority list and from there you can work to support the individual. The areas can be under headings such as vocabulary, social skills, turn-taking and so on.

Build their general vocabulary

Choose around five or six new words per week. Look at an essay the student has written and identify words they use frequently, but which are a little childish. Introduce them to alternative, more elaborate words they could replace them with, for example, replace *nice* with *fabulous*, replace *bad* with *appalling* and so on. The idea is that for that whole week, they get as much exposure as they can to those words.

- Challenge them to use them in anything they write that week.
- Get them to read passages and find where these words are.
- Repeat stories and encourage the student to use the new words as they tell the stories.
- If you are just chatting and you see an opportunity to use this word, use it.
- When you are introducing new words, model saying them. Get them to say the words back to you, but not in isolation.
- Use the words in sentences, in different contexts. Linking the words to real-life examples means they can see how the word relates to their own world. Linking the word to similar words they have already acquired is also very useful.

Check their understanding of words as you are casually chatting.

- Maybe you are just watching the TV. You hear a word you are fairly sure they don't know. Pause the TV, ask them if they know what it means and get them to explain it to you. If they are able to explain it, great; if they don't, this is a real-life learning example. Do this often.

- Encourage them to stop you when they don't know a word and ask you to explain it. Praise them for stopping you to explain a word.

There are lots of other ways to help build their vocabulary:

- Create a culture in your home or classroom where language and vocabulary-building are active.
- Talk and converse a lot with them.
- Encourage them to keep a little notebook for their own personal vocabulary bank.

Develop their expressive language

Rehearse and deliver a speech

This is as much about confidence as it is about language. It is about helping the child to find their voice and not apologise for it. Rehearse, rehearse, rehearse. Give the child something to say or read and go over it repeatedly with them. Give them loads of time to rehearse it, then give them the opportunity to deliver it in front of a small group of people they trust. This process needs to be well-rehearsed before their self-confidence is built up.

Play language games

Practising vocabulary can be great fun when you are playing language games. *Taboo* is a really good game where you have to find different ways of explaining common objects. *Describe the X* is another good game where children are given a topic and they have to describe it for twenty seconds. The other team members have to figure out what they are describing.

Encourage them to use more sentences

Answers being too short is such a common issue for many students, and not just those with speech and language difficulties. You will need to explicitly tell your child or student that they need to move on from using one-sentence statements to more descriptive and longer statements. Instead of just one sentence such as 'It is a nice day', tell them you expect five sentences describing the day. If they are talking about a person or place or event, they need to expand, expand, expand. They will need a scaffold for this, for example they can do it by using:

- *The five Ws and one H*: *Who* is she? *What* does she look like? *When* did it happen? *Where* was she? *Why* was she there? *How* many others were there?
- *Their senses*: to support making sentences longer. When describing a place, encourage them to say what it *looked* like. What *noises* were there? Were there any *smells*? What did it *feel* like? Was there food? What did it *taste* like?
- *A start, middle and end*: If they are telling stories, encourage them to have a start, middle and end. What is happening? Then what happened? How did it end?

Use listening strategies

When we need a child to listen, we may have to call their name directly, so they know we are expecting them to fully listen and engage in active listening. Teachers who know they have children with verbal comprehension difficulties need to use cues and eye contact to alert or remind them to re-engage if they have drifted off.

The following strategies allow the child to practise their listening skills effectively:

- Get the child to listen to a story and repeat back the general gist of it.
- Get the child to listen to a set of instructions and then repeat them back.
- Give the child the words of a song with some blanks for missing words, play the song and get them to listen attentively to find the missing words.
- Give the child the written version of a story with some blanks for missing words, play an audio version of the story and get them to listen attentively and fill in the blanks.
- Give the child a list of questions about a film clip and get them to watch the film clip and listen for the answers.

Work on oral comprehension

Sometimes students understand what is being said, but it is coming at them far too fast for them to process. If you give them five instructions, you may find the student looking at you blankly. However, if you give each instruction one at a time, they have no difficulties. You have just established, therefore, that it isn't the vocabulary that is the difficulty: it's the number of instructions being hurled at them all at once. This may of course be linked to processing speeds and working memory. Regardless of the underlying cause, the way to work on this is to build up the skill little by little. Establish if they can manage three instructions at a time, or if the point of overload is just two instructions. Whatever the limit, practise increasing that a little more. Children may find visual cues very helpful, and they can be used as a support, but let's face it, no employer is going to give them visual cues later in life. Students will need to come up with their own mental visual cues in order to remember things.

This can be fun to practise:

- Give the student three or four pieces of information and get them to create a visual in their head for each point. Then get them to repeat each piece back to you. Ask them if this strategy has worked.
- Record a simple story and jumble the sequence of events in the story (No more than five or six sentences). Ask them to sequence the story. This will get them to actively listen, but it will also allow them to practise the skill of sequencing. What is the start? What is the middle? What is the end? What happened first? What happened then? How did it end?

'Do you understand?' is a question to be avoided if you are checking for understanding. Instead use something like: 'Can you repeat back to me three pieces of information in relation to what we have just discussed?' This would give you a greater sense of their verbal comprehension.

When teaching something new, it is essential to break it into chunks. Teach, check, teach, check. Link back to former learning: 'That's a bit like X isn't it?' Get them to find images to go with the piece of information you are imparting. This makes the learning active and visual.

Help them to recognise distractions

Engage the child/student in figuring out how they could become better listeners. Get them to decide for themselves that sitting away from distractions might help. This prevents the them from feeling that they are being punished by being moved away from the window or up near the teacher. They may now see it as support, as the request came from themselves.

Use role play

Have a discussion about what a good/bad listener looks like. Get them to role-play a good listener and a poor listener. Get them to listen to ten pieces of information and try to recall them. Then listen to another ten pieces of information but while listening, let them jot down a word or doodle for each point (active listening) and then get them to see if it's easier to recall them. To their amazement, it will be easier.

Encourage them to take charge of a situation

Students will need to be able to stop the offending adult! This is a skill that takes a great deal of courage. It is important for a child to alert the adult when the point of saturation has been reached. Children often lose track when verbal information is coming at them too fast. Adults are not, however, telepathic. Students need to signal to the adult (teacher/parent/coach) that they need things to be slowed down. They might be confident enough to put their hand up in the class, but most schools have a traffic light system or a signal card to alert the teacher to this difficulty. This is a far better alternative than deciding to sabotage the learning by misbehaving or choosing to withdraw and then discovering they've missed out on the whole week's lesson because they didn't understand the basics of the first day. This obviously takes maturity, but there has to be an environment/culture of safely asking teachers/parents to take things step-by-step when necessary. Acquiring some of the information slowly is far better than acquiring zero information quickly.

Check their social and non-verbal language

We all know that communication is very dependent on non-verbal aspects. Children often struggle with social non-verbal communication such as appropriate eye contact and body language. Some children are far too tactile and so wreck conversations with physical inputs. They may lack self-awareness skills, such as knowing when they are talking too much or maybe realising when they are not letting others talk at all. Are they mature enough to self-assess and come up with areas of weakness themselves? Are they giving visual signals that they are listening? Can they make appropriate contributions based on that listening?

Self-awareness is also necessary for an appropriate volume of speech and social distances. You can't work on everything at the same time, and sometimes things that are not perfect don't need to be fixed, just accepted. The child only needs to be supported, if this particular area of weakness is causing them or others distress or discomfort. Is it holding them back in any way? If not, move on. However, we do need to help our children in being fit for the world they live in. Observe their social skills as they stand. Notice the areas of strength and the areas that need support. Make a priority list and choose one or two issues to work on. If you are focusing on one area, it is a really good idea to make sure school/home/clubs are all working on it together. This reinforces the skill until it becomes automated.

If social distancing is the difficulty, give them the invisible hula hoop rule as a visual. Many people may get carried away with precision and measurement; the hula hoop rule is a 'give or take a little' type of measurement and if someone gets a little closer to them, then that is OK.

If a student comes across as blunt or rude, it is rarely their intention to offend or be disrespectful. You could show video clips of someone being blunt and then discuss how that bluntness can be very easily softened by using certain words at the end of the sentence. It may be helpful to role-play an example:

- *Can I have the milk?* becomes *Can I have the milk, please?*
- *I want to go to my locker* becomes *I want to go to my locker, if that's OK?*
- *I want to get out* becomes *Can you excuse me – I need a break?*

Getting a child to see alternative (soft) ways of communication takes a lot of practice. Children also need to know that working on making their language softer is not a punishment and they are not being criticised. There will be benefits for them if they use soft language.

Overtalking

Some children have a specialist area of interest. They get taken away with passionate enthusiasm and tend to go on a bit too much. The consequence of peers telling them to 'Shut up!' or, worse still, quietly excluding them, can be very hurtful. Break it down into fractions for them: if there are three children, they only get one-third of the talk time. Inform them that one of life's social rules is to ask others some questions about their areas of interest. Of course, finding friends with like-minded interests is the ideal situation, so encourage them to try to join clubs that interest them.

Role play

Role-play how to ask questions of others and look interested, even if they are not. If social skills do not come naturally to the child, role play may feel odd. It may take some rehearsing for it to feel natural. When practising, parents and teachers should outline as often as possible what they are doing well, for example, 'You had great eye contact there. Your voice went up at the end for a question, well done!'

Volume

It is really useful to have a visual to alert the student to their volume. Too loud, a little loud, just right, too quiet.

We can never force someone to be someone they are not, but we do have an obligation to practise social rules so we can all get along well together. Keep in mind at all times that we have to accept the child we have. Only work on something that will make their life easier. Be mindful of the reasons why we are working on certain skills.

24

Social skills

Neurodiversity and learning differences don't fit nicely under distinct headings or categories. Please forgive some repetition of topics and tips discussed under the chapters on autism and language as they are also relevant under the topic of social skills support. While we may be concerned about a student keeping up with their schoolwork and achieving academic success, parents and teachers worry far more about their children fitting in with their peers. It breaks our hearts if we see a student on their own or left out, intentionally or unintentionally.

Some students have told me that they are sick of adults trying to get them to fit in and that adults fail to listen when they express that they actually like being on their own. We need to respect the true desires of students and take comfort in the fact that some students who are on their own are not depressed, isolated or dying on the inside – they are really very content. The trouble with this is that life and work require us to be social to some degree. We should not allow students to become completely isolated. As mentioned earlier, if socialising causes discomfort, we need to respect this but also explain to them that they need to desensitise themselves. They may need support, little by little, in becoming more comfortable with social interactions. They will need these skills in life, as they progress through school, college, work, relationships and dealing with independent living.

Challenges with social skills may be linked to speech differences. Often children on the autistic spectrum can come across as abrupt or clinical in their speech. This must be accepted. We must not feel the need to always 'change' our children to fit our idea of 'normal'.

SIGNS TO WATCH OUT FOR

- Being isolated at lunchtime
- Hanging back after class
- No friendship network
- Offending others with comments
- Tone coming across as abrupt or rude
- Regularly not getting the joke/idioms/sarcasm
- Inappropriate social distancing
- Limited ability to initiate a conversation
- Limited ability to show interest or respect when others are speaking
- Limited ability to engage and sustain a two-way conversation
- Poor ability to read body language
- Talking too much/too little
- Preferring the company of younger children or adults

How to help

Social skills can, however, be explicitly taught and may help the child to fit in better with society. What you decide to work on with your child needs to be examined and selected by you both.

Observe and prioritise

For some children who are on their own, the truth is they are actually dying on the inside. They have tried to fit in and have been met with rejection. In these cases, adult intervention is required. What was it that caused the rejection? Social skills are a topic that is so broad-ranging that no one chapter or book can cover it completely. Like all other issues discussed, the child's social skills should be observed. Notice their ability to:

- Request joining a group
- Initiate a conversation
- Use age-appropriate topics and vocabulary

Figure out what they are good at and what they struggle with. Keep their age in mind: we can't expect them to act as adults when they are ten. Once you have an inkling about what they are struggling with, observe again. Never make broad assumptions based on one observation. As always, once you have established what the difficulties are, pick just one or two and focus on these. If we highlight to them that they struggle in too many areas, we run the risk of ruining their self-confidence beyond repair and our name might come up in a few therapy sessions in their adulthood!

Talk to them about cool gangs and true friendship

Usually, children want to be part of the cool gang. It is important to teach children that the people who make us feel comfortable *are* the cool gang. Knowing this early on in life is fundamental. If a group makes them feel bad about themselves, then that group is a bad fit. Teach them that good friends accept them for who they are. Some students with additional needs may wish to divulge their difficulties to a group. This is up to the individual and not always necessary. However, other children may be more understanding if they know their friend has, for example, autism or maybe a hearing difficulty. They may be more accepting of perceived inappropriate statements or missing cues. Of course, children must be equipped with a few sentences to explain this. They can get themselves tied up in knots and make too big a deal out of their additional need if they have not practised this many times with a trusted adult. I have found that all children are trying to be cool themselves. They may distance themselves from someone who seems uncool, but once they know there is an additional need, they are fantastically accepting, and the additional need is then no longer an issue. The friendship can progress. Children do not need charity friends – they need friends who accept them for who they are and who enjoy their company.

Teach them the basics

There is also a need to be realistic. We have the right to surround ourselves with the company we enjoy. If someone is constantly interrupting us, pushing or shoving us, not listening to us or is sharp in their tone, then we will not want to be in their company. If this is the case, then it is not good enough to say, 'They need to accept them for who they are.' Everyone must learn to be polite and accept the needs and feelings of others. All children require support in understanding the demands of all in social settings.

Use role play

I will be referring to role play throughout this chapter. When I say role play, this is not the role play that takes place in a drama class. It is role play at any given learning moment in the home or classroom. Here is an example. When you shout out 'Dinner is ready' and repeat it five minutes later, and your children reply, 'I heard you the first time', this is rude. So what do you do?

Well, the reality is if you pull your child up on everything, you will end up damaging your relationship. It is so important to note that letting them get away with what is perceived in society as disrespectful or impolite is not doing them any favours in the long run. If, for example, your child is very abrupt or literal and this is their additional need, then you need to highlight to them that this is experienced by others as rude, even if their intention was not to offend or be insulting. The child might point out that they had been busy and were only stating the fact that they had 'heard you the first time already'. Here is where you have to fake a smile and say you are going to rewind and practise doing it correctly together:

Parent: Dinner is ready.
Child: I just have to finish this. I'll be there in five minutes.
Parent: OK.

Explain to them that this would have saved the offence created by the response 'I heard you the first time'.

Be warned that building most social skills requires persistence and for you to keep chipping away at it constantly.

Role play can also be used to soften language until it becomes more automated. As previously discussed, some students' additional needs present with an abruptness in their tone. We have addressed that using a simple 'please' at the beginning or end of a statement is very powerful in taking the abruptness out of things. Again, this will need lots of role play: catch an example of abruptness, provide an alternative statement they can use that is less abrupt and ask them to rewind and play it out again.

Use television

Watching telly is one of a child's favourite things to do. So of course, as parents, we are duty-bound to spoil it by making it a 'learning experience'! If you are trying to get your child to learn body language, it is so useful to take their favourite drama and watch it with them. There will be hundreds of opportunities for you to pause the programme and ask them, 'How do you think that character is feeling from the way they are folding their arms/frowning/holding their head?' There will be hundreds of examples of someone being kind by opening a conversation with a simple 'How are you?' You will be able to freeze the frame and ask, 'How do you know if this person is really listening?'

The first step is to observe and be able to identify all the different kinds of social cues and body language messages. The second step is to replicate them. You will need to model this. Mimicking an actor may seem a bit alien and you will feel a little silly, but once you get your child in the habit of doing this, it is actually a fun activity. The best way to learn anything is to do it on the spot as it crops up in life. This is also an activity that is simple to bring into the classroom if you are explicitly teaching social skills.

Teach them how to start and engage in a conversation

Joining a group and initiating conversations is a skill that can be modelled and copied. Equip your child with a bank of 'go-to' lines:

- Do you mind if I join you?
- What games are you interested in?
- Do you play any sport or are you in any club?
- Did you get the English homework finished last night?
- Who has a dog?
- Do you support a football team?

Discuss the things that are in their lives and create a bank of opening questions they could use when joining a group of friends.

It's one thing to ask people questions, but if they don't listen to their answers, well, they will struggle socially. Teaching them how to be a good listener starts with their knowing what a good listener looks like. Get them to notice how eye contact is held and then act it out with them or request it when you are talking to them. Give them positive reminders prior to a social interaction such as 'Remember to hold eye contact' and 'Nod to signal to your friends that you are listening'. After social interactions, highlighting failures to hold eye contact is interpreted by the child as you constantly showing disapproval and basically attacking them. It is better to give reminders *prior* to social interactions. It may seem like you are nagging but it will focus their mind and come across as supportive nagging rather than a personal attack after the event.

If a child is prone to blurting out and interrupting, then they may need specific boundaries. General statements such as 'Don't talk too much' or 'Let others talk' are too vague. If they are constantly asking questions in a classroom scenario, give them clear boundaries around what is appropriate. Tell them they can ask only three questions, so they should use them wisely. Give them advice such as, 'Remember to ask each member of the group at least one question' and 'Remember to show you are interested in their answer by using your body language'. These things come naturally to most children, but, for some, it requires explicit teaching and practice.

Teach them about sarcasm and idioms

As you watch scenes on TV together, pause the programme and check that your child understands when a person is being sarcastic. Ask questions such as, 'When he said "nice dress", did he really mean he liked the dress or did he mean the opposite?'

When different idioms come up as you go about your daily life, check if your child understands them. Each country and localities have different phrases and sayings. These may have to be explicitly taught.

- He'll be back in jig time – he'll be back soon.
- She's right as rain again – she's well again.
- I wanted the ground to swallow me up – I was embarrassed.

Even if they haven't a clue what the idioms mean, get them to guess. People who are literal are usually very logical, and given time they will figure it out.

Help them to avoid over-talking

Many students who have an additional need can be immature in relation to their peers. As mentioned earlier, they may need gentle encouragement to reduce the amount they talk about a certain topic, for example a video game or a television programme such as *Thomas the Tank Engine*. Some students may have a topic that they have become an expert on or have become overly fascinated with. This needs to be identified also. If it is not excessive and doesn't seem to annoy others, then it's not a problem – let them enjoy displaying their knowledge. However, if it appears to bother others or prevents them from having their share of the talk time, then the issue will need to be addressed. It is best if the student can identify the problem themselves and then work on it themselves with support.

As discussed in Chapter 23 on speech and language, try to observe your child's communication. Are the words they are using immature or babyish for their age? If so, you may need to embark on a programme that widens their vocabulary and use it in real-life settings, and not just when you are sitting down 'doing your lessons'. Language is a living thing. The more they practise using their new 'big' words in real-life settings, the more they will use them going forward.

Model with your own behaviour

With all this focus on what they 'should do', it is easy to see how parents and teachers can become a child's biggest critic as opposed to their biggest cheerleader. Self-esteem can be damaged, even if it is with the purest and kindest of intentions. It is sometimes useful to point out your own failings. When you say something that is abrupt or rude, don't be afraid to say, 'Gosh, the way I said that was a little abrupt. How do you think I might have said that a little more softly?' When you interrupt someone, demonstrate how you backtrack and say, 'Oh I'm sorry, you were speaking – go first, please.' Modelling is the best form of tuition. It is so basic and even seems a little old-fashioned, but if we can ensure that our children have lovely manners, they will be well-equipped for life.

25

Perfectionism

Perfectionism is often seen as a quality, something to be aspired to. Students learn very early on that handing in something perfect gains them enormous praise and high marks. If this is the standard that students set for themselves, then the only way is down. As the workload increases as they progress through school, they just won't have enough time to make everything perfect. For the average person, their best within the given time constraints is good enough – but therein lies the problem. 'Good enough' isn't perfect and, therefore, is substandard for someone who is a perfectionist. No matter what work they produce, they feel it could always be more detailed, more researched or more elaborately presented if they had more time. When we think realistically, we are only expected to do the best we can within the time constraints. Perfectionists put enormous pressure on themselves to go above and beyond what is realistically required. They see any form of advice for improvement as a sign of failure or criticism.

This difficulty of perfectionism is often, but not always, apparent in students who show signs of anxiety. It is also common with students who are on the autistic spectrum, as rigid thinking and literal interpretations of what is required generate the need for their work to be perfect.

Somewhere along the line children were told their creation or achievement was perfect and they want to live up to that expectation. In primary school years we praise students for having 'beautiful handwriting', but it may take them longer to have flowery and aesthetically pleasing handwriting. A problem may occur as they progress through to secondary school, when they are sitting exams that determine what college they might get into. There are no marks for fancy handwriting. Speed of writing becomes important. If it is legible then it's good enough.

For others, perfectionism is much more complicated and rooted in mental health issues. In a world where they feel out of control, handing in 'perfect' projects and coursework is something they can be in control of, even if it comes at the cost of burnout and high anxiety.

Signs to watch out for

- *Poor time management*: Students may become so engrossed in getting one particular assignment perfect that they simply run out of time to do the work for the rest of their subjects. They may also stay up very late studying or set the alarm clock way

too early so that they can put in more work in the morning.
- *Being emotional and, on occasion, hysterical*: When they realise they have run out of time, the student may simply panic or become overwhelmed.
- *Feeling ill*: The anxiety associated with perfectionism may lead to tummy upsets and headaches.
- *Taking teacher comments too seriously*: Teachers may make a throwaway comment like 'this class isn't working hard enough' or 'I'm expecting everyone to get an A'. These general comments made to the whole class may be taken to heart by the individual perfectionist, who definitely is working hard enough.

How to help

- *Time management training*: Students who are prone to perfectionism need support in dividing out their time between their subjects and sticking to that timetable. They need to be trained to think: 'Getting all the topics finished is more important than having one topic perfect.'
- *Praise*: Students should still be rewarded and commended for work that is really good. Statements such as 'This isn't up to your usual standard' need to be avoided. Perfectionism can simply be the will to gain praise and approval.
- *Working with peers*: Perfectionists often work in isolation, oblivious to the work of their peers. It is important to create opportunities for students to discuss their work together. They will listen to the fact that their peers may have spent only two hours on a particular assignment while they spent the

whole day. The hope is that they will subsequently lower their standards a little and not be as hard on themselves. They may listen to other students who don't take it all so seriously and, hopefully, begin to take themselves less seriously in the process. Peers will always be more influential on a student than a nagging adult.

- *Opportunities for fun*: Ensure your child or student is engaging in sporting or social activities. Most children are good at arranging to see their friends but some children may need support with this. Remind or encourage them to connect with friends. For younger children, you may be able to arrange the meet-up. With teenagers you may have to encourage them to text or make the phone call. Both as a teacher and parent, once in a while it is good to arrange fun activities that are not rooted in academics, like board games, card games or drama games. Ask them what they would like to do as a treat or for fun. Let them come up with some ideas. The best games are the ones they have learned somewhere else, where they share with you how to play them.

26

Study skills

The primary school years are predominantly spent learning how to read, write and answer questions; the problem of how to study doesn't really arise until students reach their teenage years. Parents will often say to me, 'He doesn't know how to study.' Students in primary school do lots of projects and this is one of the best forms of study they can do, so you should assure them that they do know how to study very effectively. Sitting in their room for hours, simply reading text-books, is not effective studying.

GETTING THE BASICS RIGHT

Everything comes back to the basics of:

- Enough sleep
- Diet
- Exercise
- Organisation

We have discussed these in previous chapters but they are the pillars to learning and therefore need to be referred to again. A child simply cannot study effectively if they are tired because they are up late at night on a device. They cannot study effectively if they are sluggish because they have consumed too many sugary drinks or too much greasy food or they just did not move that day. If their study space is a mess, their head will feel like a mess and they'll lose time finding bits of paper or books. They should use one dedicated workspace and it should be tidy, with dedicated storage shelves and easy access to their folders. It is essential that they have a tidying-away routine at the end of each day.

Study needs to have a purpose

Human beings don't just wander around aimlessly. If we are out for a walk, we usually have a destination or an aim of getting fitter. If we are shopping, we have something in mind we want to get. Similarly, effective study requires a purpose. These purposes are often called 'learning objectives' or 'goals' by the teachers. Teachers should always state to students something like, 'At the end of this session, I would like you to be able to tell me about X, Y or Z.'

Self-directed study will require the student to say to themselves, 'Today I'm studying this chapter and at the end of it I should be able to ...'. This is where they may encounter a hurdle. It's difficult for students to figure out for themselves what they should be able to do. We are asking them to act beyond their maturity level. The following pieces of advice should be given to them to support effective study – studying with purpose.

How to help

Look at the questions at the end of each chapter

It is best to read the questions at the end of each chapter before embarking on studying a chapter, as this will focus their minds and alert them to important pieces of information as they read. If the student can answer the questions either orally or in writing at the end of studying a chapter, they are studying effectively.

Read through past exam papers (for older students)

Highlight all the short questions and long questions that have come up on this topic. Now they can embark on their study. If they can answer these either in written form or orally, they are in business.

Turn headings into questions

Prior to studying a chapter, turn each heading into a question. The heading 'The formation of a volcano' becomes 'How are volcanoes formed?' 'Causes of World War II' becomes 'What were the main causes of World War II?' After they have read the chapter, they should check if they can answer these questions.

Understand the benefits of recall

At the end of each study session, I advise that students check if they can recall the information in either verbal or written form. I would usually tell them that what goes in must come out. If they simply read information, they will remember very little of it a week or two later.

The action of recalling it immediately has two benefits. Firstly, it will be a hook for their memory and they will be able to recollect the information better a week later. Secondly, they will discover what they don't know. We all read things and as our minds wander we may realise we haven't a clue of what we have just read. Students will often say they did two hours of study, but when you quiz them on it, you may find they can't recall anything. It's far better to do twenty minutes of focused study than hours of mindless reading.

Check for learning

Remember, we are dealing with young children or teens who have the additional complication of a learning difference. Expecting them to check their own progress after they have studied is an unrealistic expectation of maturity. An adult will need to set that expectation of checking for learning. You can do this by being their sounding board. Get them to read the chapter questions, then study, then come back to you and let you call out the chapter questions. They then answer them. Now, you may not have a clue about what they are telling you, but the process of regurgitating information is an important one. If they can't answer a question, then you could help them find that relevant piece of information. Getting them to write it down has the added bonus of creating revision notes for a later date. This process of writing is obviously difficult for some students and below, we will discover there are some fun ways around this as well. The main thing to remember is that the student will not automatically know how to study effectively. We cannot expect maturity from children. Students with learning differences are often a little more immature than their peers. They need to be shown the above strategies. They may need to have these strategies modelled, practised and rewarded.

Use projects as a study tool

Young children love doing projects, but so do big children! A student could decide to do a project on each chapter of a textbook. Some students like to write and draw, or make fancy scrapbooks and large A3 posters with fabulous mind maps and flow diagrams. Most prefer to stick to assistive technology, using whatever presentation software is popular or supported by the school. They should look again at the questions at the end of the chapter or the headings on each page and create headings for each slide. You as a parent or teacher could scaffold this process at first by creating the slide headings for them. Persuade them to summarise the information from their textbook or indeed use multiple sources – other books, interviews or the internet. Tell them it is important that each slide has a relevant image to go with it. Get them to choose one keyword from each point and put it in bold text. Students can be as creative as they like. Once they have made the slides, they can create a voiceover for them.

Of course, you will need to set some time boundaries, as they can get carried away at the expense of other subjects. This method appeals to all learning styles. The children who like to learn visually get to choose appropriate images. The children who learn aurally get to say and hear the text. Children who like to 'do' are 'doing' the project. As mentioned above, we all need a reason for doing things. Creating a lovely presentation gives them a sense of purpose. 'Why?' seems to be every child's favourite question.

Students get very good at producing projects, but make sure they are familiar with the appropriate structure. Remind them to keep the subject in mind and not get side-tracked by interesting but irrelevant topics. Get them to be mindful of the questions they are likely to be asked. Make sure they understand the need for:

- An introduction
- A minimum of three or four main pieces of information
- A conclusion or summary

Get them to include links to appropriate YouTube videos and relevant images.

We all know that the internet is super when it comes to research, but you will need to double-check that your child isn't just cutting and pasting information from the internet onto the Word document or presentation slide. We all look for shortcuts. Children won't have the maturity to understand that the process of putting things in your own words means you will remember them better in the future. This vital point must be explained to them. Make sure they know why they need to make the information their own. Putting things in their own words will also teach them that cutting and pasting is plagiarism and something to be avoided. They will need support with this. Explain how the process is more important than the product. Understanding the information is key. Anyone can cut and paste, or simply transcribe, but putting it into your own words or summarising it means you are engaging and therefore understand it. This, however, will not happen with children overnight. You may feel as a teacher or parent that you are having the same battle over and over again. Be patient but keep insisting that cutting and pasting is not an option. Keep reminding them that putting the information into their own words is to truly study.

Computers and assistive technology

Computers are not just for finding and presenting information; they are also a fantastic tool to check for understanding. After each chapter, see if you can find some online quizzes that they can do on the topic. This reinforces their learning. YouTube clips are fantastic for either visually pre-learning a topic or revising a topic after it has been studied. Put the words 'for children' in the search engine after the topic, for example, 'global warming for children'. If you don't do this, you may find you have seated them in front of material that most post-doctoral students would find difficult.

Let the students search for digital mind map apps to see which ones they like. These can be used to capture what they have learned. They can use the voice-to-text facilities to speed up the process.

There are a phenomenal number of amazing apps available that support students in learning. It is far too difficult for me to give a list of apps I find useful as the suitability of the app is so individualised. Link with your school or clinician, such as occupational therapist or psychologist, to see which apps they recommend. As a teacher you need to investigate an app's appropriateness for the particular needs of your students. Check with parents or other teachers and seek out online review groups for advice. There's no point spending hours on an app that isn't fitting for your student's/child's curriculum.

Use flash cards

Flash cards, with a question on the front and the answer on the back, are both fun for children to make and to study with. Making them engages the student in the content. These can be handmade or digital. The flash cards are then saved and are available again at the end of the year for revision.

Use study guides and summary notes

There are study guides and summary notes available to purchase in bookshops or to borrow in libraries. These support the curriculum. From the Irish perspective at secondary school level, the Revise Wise and Rapid Revision series are very popular. Parents and teachers could save their children/students lots of time by sourcing the most appropriate resources for them.

Learning from mistakes

Students need support in this area. We should remember that students, generally speaking, have not reached maturity. They see a mark from the teacher on their paper and it gets put in the bag and eventually squashed to the bottom! It is good practice to see if you can get the student to look at the teachers' comments and feedback. To engage with it. Agree with them or challenge them on it. They will need to be shown that feedback is not a putdown or criticism. It is advice that they can learn from. It can be their challenge. Of course, teachers need to be kind in their remarks. Old-fashioned, strict approaches are counterproductive and damaging. A skilful teacher or parent will not simply hand the answers to a student. They will encourage them to find the answers themselves and therefore avoid being a passive learner.

Learn to keep steady – encourage a growth mindset

When settling down to study, students may feel overwhelmed. Students who do not handle pressure well will need support in seeing that they can do the work bit by bit. They need to adopt what is popularly known as a growth mindset. Pointing out previous success is useful: 'Remember when you couldn't do [such and such] but you took your time and you did it.' Support them in staying positive. 'Only do this bit tonight and that will be enough.'

We need to instil the idea that their best is always good enough, but it should not bring them to any sort of breaking point. If they don't understand something, support them in being problem-solvers. Suggest they take a ten-minute walk, then go over the chapter again and see if they can understand it more easily with a clear head. If they still can't figure something out, could they possibly leave that section and move on to the next? Could they email a friend or the teacher to figure out the bit they are finding hard?

The emotional brain can get a bit hysterical at times, so children will need support in taking charge of it. Point out that there is always a solution and sometimes moving on to the next section or subject is the answer. Get them to mark the bit that caused them distress and get the teacher or a friend to explain it to them the next day. Once the pressure moment has passed, for example the next day or week, revisit that moment with your student or child. Remind them that our emotional brain can get us into a right state sometimes. Ask them to remember that it all turned out OK in the end, so if it happens again they should feel more in control. The calm logical brain should be able to give them a more mature response.

Use to-do lists, prioritising and study timetables

In the run-up to exams, students need to logically split up their time. Help them to build in buffer zones that will allow for unexpected events such as family or friends calling over. Make sure they include lots of relaxation and exercise times.

They need to ask themselves:

- How many subjects do I need to study (e.g. 8)?
- How many chapters are in each subject and what is the total (e.g. 32)?
- How many days are there before the exams start (e.g. 28)?

Remind them that the final few days need to be kept aside for revising all their notes again. So now they are down from 28 to 25 days. Take one buffer day per week to allow for relaxation or to make up for unexpected visitors or events. Now they're down to 21 days.

If they studied two subjects per evening (two chapters), they should be able to fit it all in. Some chapters will be longer than others but there is extra time to allow for those with this schedule.

This planning will prevent panic. If they decide to start the revision of all 32 chapters a fortnight before the exams start, it simply won't fit and they'll just be skimming and cramming it all in.

Get them to make a timetable or help them with it. Try to stick to it as much as possible. Point out that there is lots of buffer/relaxation time for them to enjoy.

Use study groups

It's a very mature thing to set up your own study group. Children may need a little help with this. Organised study groups can be very beneficial: when students get stuck, they can help each other out. This has saved many households from all-out meltdowns.

Sharing the workload is one major benefit. Students can decide that they will divide up a chapter and provide presentations to each other on each topic. They end up being an expert on their topic and will learn the other topics in a much more memorable way, as they watch their friends give their presentations. Students can show off their talents; some are dramatic, some are techie, some are meticulous. They can all learn from each other and set good realistic standards.

Stay connected

Most children are very social and well-connected – maybe even too connected. On the other hand, some are not connected and will need help with this. They may miss out on deadlines because they haven't been involved in the banter about it: 'Did you get that in yet?', 'What in yet?' or 'Did you find that difficult?', 'No, because I looked up this website ... here, have a look.' These connections with our peers help us to progress.

Students with learning difficulties may need a little help with getting into the appropriate class social media/online platforms their class is using. Many schools have an online learning platform. For the students with learning needs, teachers will have to give a little extra support in ensuring they are logged in properly and know the correct steps to upload and download work. This should not be taken for granted. The many facilities on these platforms keep children connected and up to date with what's new and helpful. It is a really useful exercise to make sure parents also know all the ins and outs of the platform; they should be able to log on and help students see what is due or what they need to look at. Schools should provide parents with this service, but if they don't, YouTube has everything about everything. Don't be afraid to engage in some self-directed learning. Better yet, get your child to explain it to you. Once it has been explained, you will need to practise using it. Remember, like all practical skills, use it or lose it!

How to study

Students can get side-tracked by online this and that, apps, pencils, study cards and random stationery. You can support your child in getting organised, but ultimately, they need to knuckle down and do the actual study. One way or another, they will need to settle down to study at some point. Too many students just sit and read mindlessly and then tell their parents they have studied for hours. Like with most things in life, quality is more important than quantity. When they have their study timetable/schedule organised, they will need to stick with it and have an 'I can do this bit by bit' attitude.

Six-step approach

Here's a six-step approach they can follow:

1. Read the questions that the teacher has set for you. Read the questions at the back of the chapter or what has come up on past papers.
2. Settle on which chapters to do first. Always start with the subject that is the hardest or that you like the least. It is best to tackle these with a fresh mind.
3. Start reading. Stay focused. Whisper – reading really quietly is an excellent way to employ another sense: your hearing. Highlight keywords or phrases.
4. After highlighting, rewrite the words into a study notebook, computer document or mind map.
5. Look at the list of keywords, phrases or mind maps. See if you can explain a bit about each to someone else or better yet, out loud to yourself.
6. Now without looking at the keywords, document or mind map, see if you can answer the questions you looked at in step one. (It is important to follow through on this fully. Train your student/child to write out the answers or say them out loud to themselves or a parent.)

Tips on highlighting

Sometimes they may not own the book, so they can jot down the keywords or phrases in a specific study notebook instead. Remember, it's not a colouring competition. They must choose only the important words and phrases to highlight. This in itself engages the mind and makes them study with purpose.

The reason for highlighting keywords is so that they'll have the ability to recall them at a later date. Bringing these words or phrases back to mind should trigger a paragraph of information for them to explain and expand.

Create one-page summaries

The main thing is to ensure the information is condensed into a short one-page document. This document then acts as a trigger once they glance over it again the following day, week or month. Compiling a book or digital folder of these notes is excellent support on the day or in the hours before exams.

Some students really like creating mind maps or graphic organisers to summarise/condense information. There are lots of free templates online. Students should choose a template that appeals to them – choosing one they like themselves is a worthwhile exercise. When transferring the information into the sections of the mind map, they should remember that it is about *condensing* and not simply *rewriting*. Adding graphics or doodles that are relevant to the keywords brings the mind map to life and makes it much more memorable when using it again for revision.

Memory tricks

Unfortunately, most educational institutions require students to sit end-of-term or year-end exams. We are moving towards a more sophisticated system where continual and class-based assessments are given greater recognition. Understanding and using information is far more beneficial than the ability to hold information in our heads for a short period of time, regurgitate it in an exam and then forget it thereafter. However, to achieve qualifications, we need to employ some memory methods. The popular ones are:

- Mnemonics
- Visualisation
- Loci method
- Brainstorming

The best memory methods are the ones students come up with themselves. There are many variations of these methods and ultimately, they need to explore what works for them.

Mnemonics

While studying, students will have compiled a list of keywords or phrases. They will need to take the first letter from each of these words, say about twenty, and make up a word using these initial letters. They can recall this word in the exam centre and, hey presto, this should trigger twenty pieces of information. For example: the wives of Henry the VIII. **A**ragon, **B**oleyn, **S**eymour, **C**leves, **H**oward, **P**arr. **All Boys Should Come Home Please.**

Visualisation (the mind's eye)

If you give a student a long list of words to remember, such as *dog*, *cat*, *what*, *ambitious*, *hammer* and so on, the words they'll recall easily are the ones with a visual. *Cat* and *hammer* give us an instant picture in our heads, but *ambitious* or *what* do not. Get children into the habit of visualising information as they learn it. If it's a person in history, get them to picture the person. If it's a volcano, picture it. If it's maths, visualise it with a real-life example. This then acts as a hook and helps them to avoid mindless reading of a text.

Some students write keywords and phrases onto small coloured index cards or Post-its. They might use different coloured pens and put boxes around the different parts. They study the card and take mental images of it, which they try to recall in the exams.

Loci method

Loci means *places* in Latin. Take that same list of keywords and phrases we've discussed. Get students to imagine they are heading into a familiar place, for example their sitting room. At the front door they place an object (that is relevant to the first keyword), then they move into the hall and behind the door they place or see the second object (relevant to the second keyword) and so on. This won't suit everyone, but some students find it really helpful.

Brainstorming

At the end of a study session, they should try to jot down as many 'bits' of information as they can – just the keywords or phrases that will jog their memory to create longer paragraphs in an exam setting. This brainstorm can then be repeated when actually required in the exam. When a student is writing their exams, they can often forget to put in information. They know it but have just forgotten to add it. Using the brainstorming method of jotting down all the relevant bits before they start answering the question is very important. As each 'bit' is explained and expanded, it can be struck off the brainstorming list. The student then works their way through the list and therefore they're unlikely to leave anything out.

27

Dealing with exams

The priority is protecting mental health and we should always remember this. Assure the student that it is only an exam and the result says nothing about how kind or how healthy they are or what they are like as a friend, etc. No exam can measure these qualities. As mentioned previously, they need to know that their best is good enough.

BEFORE THE EXAMS

Remember the basics

As mentioned before, students need to be supported to eat well, sleep well and take some exercise prior to each exam.

They will have to pack the equipment that they need. Stationery, a calculator and subject-specific equipment all must be packed the night before and ticked off a checklist before leaving the house.

Find out if they are entitled to assisted reading or any other type of accommodation during exams. Check with the student to make sure they would find this type of accommodation helpful.

Practise reading exam papers

Give students lots of practice at reading exam questions, and look out for simple things that could trip them up. If a question tells them to 'Answer A or B', point out that lots of students lose marks by not reading the 'or' and end up wasting time by answering both A and B. The examiner, however, can only mark one of them. Students can also get tripped up on instructions such as 'Answer one question in Section 1 and one question in Section 2.' They may see three questions in Section 1 and attempt all of them. With all the time this takes up, they never get to Section 2. Students need to have lots of practice doing past exam papers.

Rehearse timekeeping prior to the actual exams. Let us say they have two hours in which to answer four questions. They need to allow time for reading the paper at the beginning and checking it over at the end. There is no way of knowing exactly how much time they need unless they practise with past exam papers, as reading pace varies between students. They then divide the remaining time by four. Each exam will require a different calculation of time distribution. Get students into the habit of keeping an eye on the clock or their watch every now and then.

Don't miss the hints!

If the exams the student is studying for are in-house exams as opposed to state exams, then the last class with their subject teacher prior to the exam will include lots of hints about what will be on the exam paper. Encourage them to listen attentively in this class and focus on these topics intensively. Get them to adopt the habit of jotting down the topics of what the teacher has mentioned in the last class and use these notes as *a go-to* when they are studying.

Double-check exam timetables

Prior to the exams, students with learning differences will need you to double-check exam timetables. It's all well and good to say that you want them to be independent learners and not rely on adults, and that's fine for everyday schooling, but if the exams are important, parents and teachers will need to be absolutely sure that they have the right times and dates. Students with dyslexia and dyspraxia, for example, may struggle with timekeeping and reading dates. We know this is their area of weakness, so let's support them. Missing an important exam is too harsh a lesson for them to learn. Support them in double-checking times and dates and get them to put reminders into their diary and phone, etc.

Ask for deadline alerts

Home–school cooperation will assist the student. Most schools now have an online platform where overdue assignments are visible. If you require support in learning how to use the platform, enlist the help of your child. They are usually the best teachers. If your son or daughter isn't willing to show you how to use the platform, then the school will be more than happy to help. If there is no online platform, ask if it would be possible to get an email or private message about any important deadlines for assignments that are coming up. Where possible parents should be alerted if a child has not been submitting assignments that are due. This is not asking too much. Students with learning differences require and are entitled to a certain amount of differentiation. We need to make them responsible and self-accountable, though this has to be balanced with the reality that their lack of punctuality, frequent missing of deadlines, etc. may not be put down to being 'lazy' or 'bold', but rather down to the way their mind works. Sometimes just knowing that there is home/school communication is motivation enough for a student to ensure they meet the deadlines. Missing deadlines may also have the important role of informing us that the work is overwhelming for the student and the teacher needs to differentiate it either in terms of content or quantity. It alerts us to the fact that they require support, which they are entitled to have.

DURING THE EXAMS

Relax and read carefully

Students need to be encouraged to relax, breathe and take the exam paper bit by bit. They need to read all of it. Whisper reading is really helpful here (reading under your breath). If it's done correctly, they won't disturb the others around them.

Understand what is being asked

Once they have read all of the paper and chosen which questions they are going to do, they will need to read each part of each question again carefully and understand what is being asked. During house exams, if a question doesn't make sense to them, they should ask for it to be read to them. Now is not the time to be shy or worry about what people will think. The teacher/supervisor may or may not be entitled to read it out for them but there is no harm in asking. During state exams, the student will only be able to ask for a question to be read if the accommodation has been previously requested and granted (please see the section on accommodations).

Identify the main parts of each question

Encourage them to use a highlighter to mark the main parts of the question. Some questions can be wordy so they will need to break up the question. There may be three questions rolled into one paragraph, so a highlighter will be useful to point out all these parts. Get the student to number them on the exam paper and get them into the habit of checking that they have answered all parts of the question before they move on to the next question. Sometimes they can be so relieved to finish a section that their natural instinct is to move on.

Read the question carefully and stick to what is being asked

A common error that students make is to write reams of information on topics they are not asked about. Going off target is a common mistake and students need to get into the habit of stopping and reflecting after every ten minutes of writing. They should read the question again and ask themselves, 'Am I answering the question on the paper?'

Number the answers correctly

It seems obvious, but get students into the habit of numbering their answers to match the number of the question they are answering. Make it easy for the examiners to know what sections they are referring to. Marks can be lost when examiners cannot figure out what answer relates to what question.

Follow the marking scheme

Looking at the marking scheme is essential. If one question is worth two marks and another is worth ten, well, it needs to be pointed out to students that not all answers are equal. They should give more detail and time to the questions with the greatest marks.

Use and explain labelled diagrams

Encourage them to put diagrams in their answers wherever possible. Sometimes students with learning differences can find writing long paragraphs difficult, but a quick diagram can speak a thousand words. A note of caution: if a diagram isn't labelled and explained, then it's just art, isn't it? Science or Geography teachers aren't art teachers. The diagram must be labelled and explained properly in order to get marks.

Time the answers

Students need to be mindful of their timekeeping. Every exam centre will have a clock. Make sure if they are bringing their own watch into the exam centre, that it complies with rules around smartwatches as some students may get upset if their watch is taken from them prior to the exam.

Running out of time

Train students to cope with a situation where they are running out of time. Teach them to move on to the next question and just list as much information as they can in their answer. Even if they just use bullet points, they need to try and answer every question. They must not get overwhelmed and give up. It's amazing how many marks can be gained by just jotting down the main points.

Avoid blanks

Students should know that they must never ever leave a question blank or unanswered. This is especially true for types of questions with short answers. I've even seen occasions where multiple choice questions were left blank! The students won't get docked marks if they're wrong and educated guesses are often right.

Finishing early

If students are finished early, get them into the habit of checking back over the paper to make sure they:

- Have answered all the required questions, so that no section is left blank
- Have answered what was being asked in the question and didn't go off topic
- Try to add more information to the existing questions (see the tip below)
- Finally, look at other sections and see if they could do another question. You never know, they might get more marks in this one than the one they originally chose

Tip: If they are finished very early, chances are that they have not written enough in their answers. So often teachers' and examiners' comments sound something like 'More detail needed' or 'Did not expand'. This means nothing to students really. If there isn't enough detail in an answer, they will need to use prompts that may produce more information. Get them to create *Who*, *What*, *When*, *Where*, *Why* and *How* questions in their mind and answer these questions on the page. Get them to think: what did it sound like, smell like, look like, taste like, feel like? This should generate more content that can be added to the answers.

Answers that demonstrate critical thinking

It's one thing to memorise and repeat information, but the student who displays critical thinking abilities related to the question will demonstrate that they really understand the topic and therefore rise above their peers. They should try to read between the lines, discussing the tone of the article or implications of certain actions of characters in a play or in history – these are the students who get higher marks. This is a much more important skill than being a good speller. Imagine how bored examiners must be reading the same things over and over again! Along comes a student who is answering their questions, but with critical thinking. Encourage them to use extended vocabulary (or, as my children say, 'big words') whenever possible. Being able to see two sides of an argument gives them twice as much to write about!

Give evidence

One thing we must train students to do is to back their statements up with evidence. We cannot simply state that maybe that villain in the story was actually kind, without confirming it with evidence: 'He showed he was kind when he did X.' Children have wonderful opinions and are fantastic at challenging and questioning, but we need to support them in backing up sweeping statements with evidence from the text. It is a specific skill that can be taught and reaps rewards in their exams.

Get students to choose quotes that appeal to them. They can learn them by heart and use them when answering questions. These are particularly useful in subjects like English, History and other social sciences.

After the exams

Get the student to enjoy the fact that the exams are over. They may want a quick chat about it; keep it positive. Try to avoid pointing out what they missed or got wrong. It's time to relax and enjoy what they have achieved. So many students get themselves into a state of anxiety when they do a post-mortem on an exam. 'I should have done this or written that' is not helpful if it is stressing the student out. A day or two later, it may be helpful to reflect and learn from the experience. Students could be asked:

- Do you feel you started studying early enough?
- Do you feel you divided your time up well?
- What did you do well?
- What would you improve on for next time?
- Is there anything you need to go over?

But, straight after the exams is a time to praise your student. Spoil and treat your child.

28

Keeping your child safe

No matter what your child's learning difference may be, you as a parent or teacher need to be mindful of the possibility that this child may be vulnerable. Many students with learning differences are far from immature and are actually very streetwise. However, some may be a little more immature than their peers. A fifteen-year-old mixing with older teens, for example seventeen-year-olds, may only have the street wisdom of a twelve-year-old – see where I'm going with this? Obviously, you cannot withdraw your child from the world they live in, so it is important to have very clear and open communication with your child or student. Reinforce the point that there is nothing that they can't come to you about.

The internet is also an area where many students have found themselves in some difficulties. Vulnerability can lie in immaturity. More often than not, getting into bother on the internet is related to innocence and lack of self-esteem, for example, by sending inappropriate pictures in the I belief that they will be accepted by their peers if they do. Saying no to strong characters takes a lot of self-esteem and courage.

Many students with learning differences excel in the area of technology. The dominance of the right side of the brain helps them here. They may find ways of getting into technology that you don't even know exist. Impulsivity may be a problem: click here and click there and God knows where they might end up.

How to help

Be very explicit about what they can and cannot do.

It may be useful to role-play scenarios, such as being offered drinks or drugs, or even sexual activity. Make sure they know the correct responses to the many possible dangerous situations.

Building this self-esteem and resilience requires lots of reinforcement from parents and teachers.

Be mindful of who their peers are. As a parent, if you feel your child is running with wolves, so to speak, then you have the responsibility to ban inappropriate friendships. A child's self-esteem can only flourish if they are among friends they feel comfortable with and who accept them for who they are. Some children need this lesson to be pointed out to them.

The internet is part and parcel of the world we live in. I would advise holding off on the use of smartphones until your child is at least twelve years old. If you need to contact your child, then consider giving them a non-smartphone. For your child's safety, you must agree prior to the purchase of the device that they share their passwords with you. Check their messages, photo gallery and search history regularly. Even if they protest, this is an 'I'm the parent, you're the child' moment!

The reality is that they will always be one step ahead of you in this field. Obviously using the latest protective software and checking their phone history are all good parenting strategies, but it will not prevent them from being accidentally exposed to inappropriate material. We as parents and teachers need to support them in developing a good moral compass. The hope is that when they are faced with inappropriate material, they learn to make good choices for themselves, self-regulate and say no to strangers online and avoid wandering onto websites they shouldn't be on. Regular communication and open discussions are the only real way to protect your child online. If they have strayed into something they shouldn't have, the line of communication with parents and teachers needs to be a supportive one. If they believe that they are going to get into huge trouble, they will be unlikely to divulge what they have done. They will fail to ask for the help and support they may need to get out of the mess they may be in.

Children complain about rules, but bizarrely, they actually like them. Many children who come from chaotic home environments despair that no one cares enough to impose rules. Subconsciously, they feel safe when they have clear rules. It gives them the excuse to say 'no' to things they don't really want to do anyway. It's always about balance. They need rules to guide and protect them, yet enough freedom to make mistakes: valuable mistakes they can learn from.

29

A final note

Being the parent or guardian of a child with additional needs is not an easy gig. The reality is that you may experience discrimination and, regrettably, some ignorance along the way. This can put some parents into a negative default or automatic fight mode: feeling that if they don't fight, then their children won't get their entitlements, and therefore won't achieve their potential. The stress of all that negative energy is simply damaging our own personal health and happiness. But we can't help thinking, are we not being the best parent we can be if we don't push, check and sometimes fight?

Please trust me when I tell you things are rapidly getting so much better. There is far greater knowledge out there now about all the different additional needs than when you were in school. More tailored differentiation and accommodation are being strived for in schools. Teachers care. It is important to really step back and look at what your child needs. Sometimes we are fighting for an 'entitlement' that will actually hinder them. Keep conversations frequent with your child and the school/parent and try to keep them positive and solution-focused.

Aim to keep the 'programmes' to a minimum. In a manic effort to do our very best to help our children reach their potential, we can put way too much pressure on them, steal a little bit of their childhood and unknowingly create an untenable amount of anxiety in our own lives. Keep the interventions realistic and, most importantly, be kind to yourself. Don't be afraid to take a break from the interventions and do some fun activities together for a little while.

In 2020 I experienced some health difficulties and suffered some serious post-operative complications. I was very sick, and in those moments it was all *so* clear. Why had I spent so much time correcting and pushing my children to 'their full potential'? Time is better spent enjoying their company and indulging in just being with them. I swore in those moments I would never give out or correct or judge again.

Now obviously that clarity didn't last too long! I've reverted back to my old ways I'm afraid. But I try to ensure now that I guide and advise rather than criticise and judge. Criticism and judgement are negative and exhausting on you both. I'm not sure I succeed, but at least I'm a bit more conscious of the need to be more gentle on my children and myself.

Thank you so much for reading this book. My heartfelt best wishes for personal happiness are being sent to you and your child.

Resources

I am reluctant to offer any parent or teacher a list of resources. The reality is that this would take away from the fact that supporting the child with learning differences should be very individualised and tailored. The needs of a five-year-old child with autism are far different from a child of fifteen with the same learning differences. The technology that supports students changes so rapidly that it can be out of date in a week!

The main resource you have, both as a parent and a teacher, is the additional needs team in your school. They will have tried-and-tested programmes and strategies that they can support and are familiar with.

There are many specific organisations and Facebook groups that offer fantastic support. Finding one in your area will provide you with advice and recommendations.

From an Irish perspective, the National Council for Special Education website, NCSE.ie, is full of wonderful resources and advice.

Understood.org is another great site with really useful articles and guidance.